Manage teams through chaos, before chaos managed you.

37 rules of effective team.

The foundation of corporate culture.

Remember, understand and adhere to the company's temperature regime in the form of three "P's" – Principles, Rules and Paradigms of Work.

Observance of all rules is the basis for the effective functioning of the company.

Peter Sinegub

Table of Contents

INTRODUCTION

Greetings, folks!

For more than fourteen years of business management, I have determined what the operating efficiency of a company depends on. In this formula, there are three summations.

◆ Professional staff.

◆ A team loyal to the company.

◆ Each employee knows the expected result of his activity.

However, you and I are well aware that professionalism, loyalty, and results-orientation do not occur at all. We have to work on them. It is therefore important for a company to agree on rules, principles, and paradigms that all employees will follow.

But what are the rules? Do you have to be on time? No swearing? Respect the chain of command? Let's dig deeper. For thirteen years, my employees and I have faced many operational errors. And it wasn't always about the little things. Sometimes mistakes entailed the loss of money, customer dissatisfaction, and other unpleasant things. The first thing we did was to solve the problem as a matter of urgency. And then I asked myself the question: what must be done to ensure that this error does not happen again in the future? That's how the 37 rules came about.

Now you are reading a book about the results of past mistakes - the corporate rules, principles, and paradigms on which a company's effectiveness depends. If a company is a state, the 37 rules are part of its constitution, laws, and regulations.

Can you imagine a self-sufficient, developing state with a high standard of living, where there are no laws? It's difficult. It just so happens that laws are the basis of any community.

At the same time, you and I understand very well that professionalism, loyalty, and orientation to the result do not arise from nothing. We have to work on them. Therefore, it is important to agree on rules, principles, and paradigms that all employees will follow.

But what are the rules? Do you have to be on time? No swearing? Respect the chain of command? Let's dig deeper. For fourteen years, my employees and I have faced many operational errors. And it wasn't always about the little things. Sometimes mistakes entailed loss of money, customer dissatisfaction, and other unpleasant things. The first thing we did was to solve the problem as a matter of urgency. And then I asked myself the question: what must be done to ensure that this error does not happen again in the future? That's how the 37 rules came about.

Now you are reading a book about the results of past mistakes - about corporate rules, principles, and paradigms on which company performance depends. If a company is a state, the 37 rules are part of its constitution, laws, and regulations.

Can you imagine a self-sufficient, developing state with a high standard of living, where there are no laws? It's a bit difficult. It just so happens that laws are the basis of any community.

The company is the same state. It can't thrive without a strong legislative framework. Nevertheless, most companies exist in this way. According to my statistics, only ten percent of small and medium business companies have a document with common rules. And employees of these companies are not always aware of the existence of such a document.

The rules explain to the employees how to behave in different working spheres and situations to be on the same wave with the company:

◆ How to perform your tasks daily.

◆ How to communicate with colleagues.

◆ How to interact with management.

◆How to move up the career ladder.

By accepting such a document in the company, we conclude a contract with employees. We promise each other that we will behave like this at work. From now on, we do not need to explain again how we delegate tasks, develop professional skills, or ask for a promotion.

The number of rules is not random. As long as employees agree with all the rules and comply with them, the corporate temperature is kept at a stable level. But as soon as there is some malfunction, the company's immunity weakens, and it gets sick.

What kind of malfunctions are we talking about? Employees sabotage or ignore the rules, and management overloads the team with additional rules. In my experience, I have found that both a lack of and excess rules create the same stress.

In the course of the book, something may seem obvious to you. I understand, but you have to communicate with respect. It's clear that you need to work effectively. It is clear that to move up the career ladder you need to demonstrate results and leadership skills.

Question: if everything is so obvious, why do the owners of small and medium businesses still have to clean up their operations? Why are they afraid to go on vacation, fearing that everything will develop without them? Why are they spraying their attention on all departments at once?

I still have a lot of "why" like that. Of course, corporate rules alone will not solve all the problems of the owner and his business at once. But believe me: this is what triggers change and closes a huge niche of management and HR-department.

Let me say more: corporate rules as if open the eyes of the owner and managers to their team. When I started implementing changes in my company, some employees left, and I fired someone myself. It turned out that some of those I worked with for years did not want to take responsibility or were not ready to accept the changes.

The same is true for the teams that participate in our Smart Business Owner training program. They implement a couple of rules and inevitably face layoffs. And you know what? That's good. It's better to reassemble part of the team and work with like-minded people. And it's a lot worse not to develop your company because of the individuals.

"He's been working here so long," and "maybe he'll get better."

37 rules are the foundation of corporate culture. I can't say it's written in blood. But certainly, with tangible monetary loss, stress, and disappointment in people. These are my mistakes, the mistakes of my companies, and other business owners who are trained by us.

In my first business, the World of Libra group of companies, there are over a hundred people. They all work in the same corporate culture, which is based on these 37 rules, principles, and paradigms.

The main purpose of this book is to show you that by implementing rules it is quite feasible to increase the efficiency of the team. In such conditions, the businessman can be engaged in its initial task - the development and implementation of the company's strategy and the development of corporate culture.

These points are universal in their meaning - they are suitable for any small or medium business in which people work. You can confidently adapt them to your reality and combine them with what is. For me, the most important thing is that you have a working point of reference which my employees and our client teams are using right now.

So, I wish you a pleasant reading and interesting conclusions!

How to Read This Book: 7 Tips from Me

Idea and implementation. As a business owner or top manager, you understand the difference between these concepts. Every second an idea is generated in the minds of some of our planet's residents. But even the most ingenious one is not worth a dollar if it has not gone beyond the head.

The book you're reading now is an idea. I'm sure it's good for small and medium businesses. But only if it jumps from these pages into your corporate rules book and becomes part of your team's daily life.

Below are some recommendations for working with this book. They will help you make reading as efficient as possible. Adopt at least some of them and it will be much easier for you to build the bridge between idea and implementation.

1. Read the book fluently for the first time. Try to understand its main idea without focusing on small details.

2. At the end of each chapter, there is a QR code that leads to a page with a short video for each rule. Look through these videos if you can. This will help you consolidate the idea of the rule and look at it from the other side.

3. Leave the chapters that you found useful for your company to go back to again. Read them slowly and thoughtfully. If necessary, make notes and write your conclusions in the margins.

4. Print out the rules you like and let the key employees and then the whole team read them first. You can put up a list of rules in a prominent place in your office.

5. Use the texts of chapters and videos from each rule in the adaptation system for new employees. This will help them to get acquainted with the corporate way of life more quickly and not make common mistakes.

6. If you have any questions or want to know more, please write to me in the social networks marked "37 rules of effective team ". This way I can see your message more quickly and help.

7. And the main recommendation: implement the rules if you are ready to follow them yourself. Be an example to your team.

Let's do it!

First rule

You know how to improve the workflow - offer!

Initiative, useful ideas, and rational suggestions are encouraged.

It's not the strongest that survives, but the most receptive to change.

Charles Darwin.

What do you think about when you hear the word "stability"? I think of greyness, silence, and boredom. You have to admit, now this notion is increasingly associated with something negative. In the past, what is expressed by the word "stable company" was the main goal of any entrepreneur. Where did the parents of our parents try to find a job? Stable production, about forty years old.

It's not quite fair to ironize over this word and deny the benefit of stability. In some respects, the company must be strong regardless of the circumstances. I am talking about regular salaries, growth indicators, acceptable working conditions.

However, in other areas, business is at great risk when it is immersed in its cozy world. As soon as there are some fluctuations in the external environment, an overly stable company feels them with the force of a ten-point earthquake. Not every brand is capable of recovering from such devastation.

One of the first businesses to realize this was Toyota. After World War II, it found a way to recover together with other Japanese companies. How? They invented "kaizen".

Kaizen is a Japanese word that is translated as "continuous improvement". In other words, Kaizen is a philosophy of continuous improvement. For management, this means that absolutely everyone in the company, from owner to cleaner, has to continuously improve his or her work process to increase personal efficiency. The Japanese have realized that fundamental changes are not always necessary. Small, but regular improvements are enough. Kaizen is now a global approach. Most business owners consciously choose the policy of continuous improvement. This is wise: to build a flexible structure in the company and to establish communication with the team so that at any moment it was possible to group and change something.

I am a supporter of this approach. It is simply impossible to develop in a competitive market in any other way. There is always someone who adapts to changes more quickly or launches them himself. Any company needs to understand that it does not exist by itself. Nearby there are always competitors who can get ahead at any moment.

But competition is not the only motivation. Owners and managers need to understand that they need to become not only better than someone but also better than themselves. Perhaps the thought is not the freshest, but it is. We are yesterday's and tomorrow's - that's who should compete.

Now let's move from philosophy to business. Let's say the company owner has decided to launch regular improvements. But where does he get them? To invent them himself. To call tops, key employees and to create with them? It seems logical. But if we are not talking about some strategic changes, top management is not the right source of ideas.

To be more effective and to increase the overall performance, the business does not have to be wise when it comes to inventing something global. Sometimes it is enough to reconsider the typical business processes of their subjects. It is a question of receiving requests from customers or delivering goods. This kind of routine is the daily work of dozens or even hundreds of employees.

With all the sincere desire to "pump up" these processes, the owner or director is purely physically unable to do it to the fullest extent. Yes, he can order an audit or become a mystery shopper. But this will give him an understanding of only external problems of the service. All "insides" will remain the same. So how do you pull them out into the light?

The only answer is to ask the process participants themselves. Yes, yes, the ordinary employees. Believe me, they know exactly what should be added and what should be removed a long time ago. They are the ones who suffer every day from unnecessary approvals, dozens of signatures, calls, and other redundant movements. It is they who have long wanted to implement a new program and purchase the necessary equipment.

Here's a trite example: the department does not have a printer. To print another document, workers distract colleagues from neighboring offices, while spending time going there and negotiating. Buying another printer and at least two departments perform their duties more efficiently. Of course, a printer is a necessity. It's been in almost every office for a long time. But let's look at it this way. Not all of us have something so obvious that every company is supposed to have. If you walk through things like a printer, a management system, a CRM - and the company will start working again. What the hell is a printer! In a western company, a cleaning lady suggested cleaning floors with a new cleaning agent because it is more concentrated and organic. The management listened to this advice. And what do you think? The company has saved a huge amount!

So, offers from the employees themselves are an effective way to increase efficiency. I've seen it for myself in practice. But a company that wants to take the initiative of a good tradition faces a new challenge: to convince the team that initiative is encouraged, not punished at all.

Unfortunately, many people are firmly entrenched in all sorts of stereotypes about making proposals. Everyone has their fear:

◆ "Colleagues will think I'm a pop-up."

◆ "The manager will make me implement everything myself."

◆ "The manager will criticize my idea."

The initiative of many people is hindered by the experience of previous jobs, where too "stable" management responded to any proposal with one phrase: "You came up with it - you do it!

Fighting the negative attitudes of each colleague is difficult. This is how business risks quickly becoming a psychological center. When I was tired of fighting a point problem, I simply launched a policy of continuous improvement and change at the corporate level. And not for nothing, but material rewards.

How does this happen? Every employee knows that the company's management expects rational suggestions from him. Their rationality is that they make the company more efficient by any means. These can be important changes in the business process or, for example, the installation of universal smartphone chargers in each office.

How can an employee bring their idea to the table and who to contact? This process is optimized. My colleagues have created a special form in the lust management system. The person opens this form and answers the template questions:

◆ What is the point of the proposal?

◆ Why should it be implemented?

◆ What benefits will it bring to the company?

The employee then forwards this information to his or her supervisor. He or she considers the idea and decides whether or not to implement it.

But! If the manager has rejected the idea, she's still entitled to consideration. The idea is passed on to a superior manager. If he does not see the potential in it, it can reach the owner of the employee considers it very important.

If the idea turns out to be worthwhile, the company implements it. And that's not all! At the monthly meeting of the author, ideas are rewarded with a prize and publicly praised. I emphasize, when colleagues see that their comrade is praised, they want to be in his place.

It is important to explain to the team exactly how this process takes place and how the reward system works. When the employees make sure that the people upstairs really expect ideas from them, they will generate them more actively. With this motivation, they will not just offer when they are "pressed" but analyze their every step and do their job more consciously.

I would not recommend this rule if I was not convinced of its effectiveness through my own experience. At Mir Weights, seventy percent of the improvements have been achieved with the help of employee suggestions. The sooner management implements this rule, the sooner the company will be more efficient.

That the rule gives

"You know how to improve your workflow," suggest! Initiative, useful ideas. and rational proposals are encouraged."

◆ Staff and management flexibility.

◆ Employee loyalty to change through developed readiness for change.

◆ Advantages over competitors: the winner is the one who is the first to adapt to change and new technologies.

◆ Continuous company development.

Second rule

Report not only the problem

Report not only on the problem but also on possible solutions.

Provide information ONLY in the "Best Option" format.

Most people don't want freedom because it implies responsibility, and responsibility most people are afraid of.

Sigmund Freud.

Tell everyone you run in the morning.

Don't make it clear what the responsibility and the problem are.

Sync by honeybunny

This rule is one of my favorites. It's a revelation to participants in our training programs and it's changing their approach to delegating tasks. I hope it will prove useful to you as well. But one thing at a time.

I started my first company in 2005. There were three of us then. You see, each of us covered many more positions than we occupied. I was a salesman in the morning, a logistician in the afternoon, and a loader in the evening. Our team did not have enough days to close all day tasks, but we somehow managed to develop business.

In such a crazy schedule I had one dream - to expand the company and hire specialists to whom I could delegate a significant part of "not my" tasks. And my dream came true - we were recruiting more and more people. I realized this when, on another weekday, I spent all my time in the office and never went out to help unload the goods.

So, I handed out the tasks to my colleagues. But what did I encounter? I was involved in their solution anyway. Yeah, technically, the task had a change in the performer. But in fact, I kept doing what other people had to do.

That's what my employees were doing:

◆ came up and asked for details of the task.

◆ would return the task to me as soon as they encountered problems.

◆ couldn't decide on their own, and they would shift it to me.

Responsibility for the task from and before is the responsibility of the executor. If every ten minutes the leader is distracted, penetrates someone else's task, and solves it, the need for such a person disappears. Why are they needed if they take time and prevent you from focusing on higher priority goals?

If you act impulsively, the first desire is to fire everyone and hire more qualified employees. And this idea disappears immediately. Everybody can't be bad employees on their own. These people have been interviewed and have proven themselves in many ways. So, what's the problem? The problem is how they report on results.

The simplest thing would seem to be to report on the results. Well, what could be more primitive? But as it turns out, it plays a significant role. Especially when you look at your watch and realize that you have spent several hours of your day doing someone else's work.

Here's what I've learned: it's not enough to just give the ward a task and say, "Do it!"

First of all, it is important to explain to him that with the task he takes responsibility for it. Just like that: "The task is on you; I'm waiting for the result".

Secondly, each employee needs to explain the form in which they should report on the work they have done. I am talking about the "best option" format.

What is this format and what is its uniqueness? The "best option" is the format for reporting on the performance of a task in which the manager only has to say, "I approve," or "I approve".

"I don't approve." What's the point? A staff member performs the assignment in such a way that the supervisor does not have additional questions or clarifications. Everything has to be clear.

These are the points the answer contains:

◆ An employee explains the task.

◆ Provides several solutions and explains why he chose them.

◆ Selects the best one among several variants and explains why it is most acceptable in this situation.

Let's say that you asked your HR specialist to find a restaurant to host a corporate event. In doing so, you listed the key criteria: district, convenient parking, capacity, etc. Here you want to finish and go about your business. An hour later, however, an employee comes to you and says: "I have gone to several places. Look, everyone is more or less walking".

What's going on? Your specialist returns the task to you and asks you to solve it for him. Yes, he seems to have done what was required of him, but only partially. If you end up choosing a good place for yourself, the employee will think: "What a good job I have done! And if the place doesn't turn out to be the best, the same employee will say, "I didn't choose it, it was the manager!"

This is how the report on the same task sounds in the "Best Option" format:

- I found three places that match the criteria you specified: this, this, and this. I think it's worth choosing the last option because this institution will still have a discount for our team.

As a result, you are only required to approve or not approve the analytical work of the employee. And most importantly, he did it himself and is responsible for his decision. Imagine how great it would be if employees solved every problem in this way!

The only thing that may not suit the manager in such an answer is an incomplete view of the picture and, consequently, the wrong decision. But here the problem lies in the initial input data. For the employee to correct his answer, the manager can give new input data.

Otherwise, the "best option" format is indeed the best I have seen in terms of delegation of responsibility. Its main advantage over other methods is that it makes team members responsible for their decisions.

Usually, how does it happen? The employee has a problem, goes to the manager, waits for his decision, and thinks:

"It turned out to be so easy! I will now always ask the manager if there is anything. There's no point in exerting pressure on myself".

It's not just about work tasks. With sudden force majeure, it's the same thing. It shouldn't be like this in a company:

- The manager, the contractor has delayed the deadline. What should we do?!

- Manager, they wrote an angry Facebook review about us.

What can we do?

- Supervisor, the goods were delayed because they were delivered to another!

When a team does not know how to solve tasks on its own, it gets attached to its manager as a nurse. The format is.

The "best option" allows to clean up this area and to train employees to be independent.

Nevertheless, "The best variant" will not cope with its task if the method is applied in one go. I felt it on myself and my team. People need to be disciplined, otherwise, they will not get used to the new rule. Even worse, they will think that it was introduced formally, but in reality, everything remains the same. It's an important point. It's worth starting with the top managers to implement this rule. First, you need to convey its value to them and only then you need to let the whole team down. Why exactly in this order? Because as long as they do not come up with questions themselves, their employees will do the same.

I introduced this rule in my company a few years ago, but so far, some department heads have not fully understood it. I can see it by the form in which they report problems to me and how they shift responsibilities. When this happens, I clearly understand that the same thing is going on in their departments.

It tells me that it's hard for people to change their habits. If you have a question about what to do with top people who have not accepted this rule for years, I answer: fire them. Some people were not appointed by me as managers because they were ideal for this position. There were other reasons: because they had been working for a long time because they had done their job well. But, as you understand, over time, such ill-conceived decisions make themselves felt.

For my team not to forget the "Best Option", I came up with this thing: to stick stickers with the name of the reception on the lid of the monitor. One for myself, the other for my colleagues.

In the end, when you or your employee is approached with a question, the sticker as if says, "Are you sure?"

And then the employee leaves to prepare the report in a new format, and the person at the computer doesn't even notice it. Time is saved.

Well, I wish you the successful implementation of this

rule and easy adaptation to it by your team!

What gives the rule

"Report not only the problem but also its possible solutions. Provide information ONLY in the "Best Option" format.

◆ Delineates roles and responsibilities between executive and manager.

◆ Unleashes the hands of the manager and allows him to focus on the strategy of the company or department.

◆ Gives employees responsibility for their decisions.

Third rule

I'm not sure - don't promise! If you promise, do it!

Consider whether what you promise is true and possible, for a promise is a duty.

Confucius

Keeping your word is a powerful tool for creating an outstanding future. We underestimate its strength and poorly use its potential. But what if you make the value of a reserved word a number one priority for your entire company?

Just think about what results you could achieve! What kind of employees would you like to be surrounded by? How incredibly simple it would be for you to work with such people!

Brian Tracy

How do we usually negotiate with partners? We conclude a contract and sign it. Each party undertakes to perform...to make sure everyone gets to the end of the day.

The company has the same system in its working relationship. Only instead of signing sealed and autographed contracts, colleagues simply set tasks for each other and perform them. It's just routine, isn't it? But what happens when suddenly some specialist does not do what he or she promised? The system breaks down.

The causes of such failures are different. The most important thing is irresponsibility. By their psychology, any person wants to show their best. That's why often an employee takes on a difficult task to prove himself - say, look, I did not lie at the interview about my golden qualities, now you will see for yourself!

But such an employee forgets that his promise in itself is just words. Without a result, it will not impress anyone.

The company is not a beauty contest, where it is enough to say:

"I'm for peace in the world," and everyone applauds. At work, real achievements are judged. That's why every promise of a task has to be complemented by a result.

I think that any business owner and manager understands the importance of performance. Without this trait, it is difficult to achieve a high position honestly. I think it's important for you that your team fulfills its work promises in the same way as you do it yourself. You do?

I'm discouraged by these dialogues with employees:

- Have you fulfilled your task?

- No, I didn't.

- Why not?

- It didn't work out...

- Then why did you promise?

- I thought I could handle it.

Has every leader ever had a conversation like this that hasn't led to anything? It's true, they don't wave their fists after a fight. The task wasn't completed anyway, the deadline was broken, the process was stalled.

It's happened more than once in my companies. And when I realized the reason for such serious malfunctions, I introduced this rule. There is no point in explaining to every "stratified" employee that this cannot be done. Yes, he'll understand, but others will remain potential violators.

The main advantage of the third rule is that it instills responsibility in the wards. The rule immediately dots the "i":

- We don't get through empty promises, we expect you to act.

Sometimes owners neglect to inform employees about their obligations. And I can see why. It's just that people in high places are already rooting for their company, they have a natural sense of duty towards everything they do. The problem is that they project their qualities onto those around them: "If I am like this, then there are just as responsible people around me".

But it doesn't always happen this way. It doesn't always happen.

No employee is in a vacuum. He works inside a system where everyone depends on each other. And his "failures" cause a lot of problems. To protect himself, the manager should explain it to the whole team.

For professionals who sometimes like to impress their promises, this will be a "stop signal". They will lose the motivation to take on tasks and not finish them off. Why, if it doesn't advance them in any way? It will most likely even worsen their situation because the leader will understand their intentions.

It has to be said that not all employees are necessarily sly. Not- who promise to do the job because they don't want to lead the manager. They understand that they lack knowledge, that they have a complete failure, that they will not succeed. Nevertheless, they promise. Only they do not take into account the fact that their "sense of duty" will still end up disappointing the manager.

I'm for honesty in working relationships. Let the employee tell me right away that he can't. In that case, I will have time to choose another performer. Later, I think about how to broaden the knowledge of this specialist so that in the future he could agree to perform a similar task. This is much better than believing and not getting results.

Many team members think that by refusing, they will destroy their reputation. So, by implementing this rule, I focused on one point:

- Do not be afraid to tell the truth. I will not fire you if you honestly admit that you cannot accomplish one task. On the contrary, I will thank you for the fact that you prevented a possible collapse in time. It is much worse for me, as it is for everyone in charge if you promise and do not.

And that helped. No one has given up their job massively just to do less. However, HR and I are trying to select "the ones" for the team. But this rule has brought a little more confidence in the relationship between each manager and the team. People realized that they are not just tools in the eyes of management.

And as long as we're talking about responsibility, I'll share a life jacket with you. I'm using it to ensure that my organization isn't used in small things, even if unintentionally. I'll explain it to you by example. The phone is ringing. I pick up the phone, and a friend of mine asks me to dump the phone of our mutual friend. I'm busy and I can't do it right now. I used to say I'd call you back in ten minutes and give you a contact.

But that's not quite right. Why not?

It's not my responsibility to find out if I need that phone number. And yet I've taken on an additional task from the outside, although I'm not chilling myself. So now, in response to such requests, I say:

- I'm busy right now. Call me back in ten minutes, please, and remind me.

Everybody. I've sifted out an extra assignment and I'm still on my own... When I'm free, I'll be sure to help - no problem dropping the number, the presentation, something to dictate, etc. But let me be reminded of this by someone who needs it. I do not want such thoughts to hang in my subconscious in the background. I advise you to have both your lifejacket and the rule. It's the little things that make up our working day. And I want there to be fewer violations, especially on such stupid occasions.

What gives the rule

"I'm not sure - don't promise! "If you promise, do it!"

◆ It teaches employees to earn respect through their work, not through their words.

◆ Removes the cult of eloquence and sets the team up for real work.

◆ Creates in employees a sense of belonging to the team, the desire to be part of the work process.

Fourth rule

Speak briefly and in essence.

Take care of your time and that of others.

It is a pity that in our society to steal someone else's time

is not as indecent as stealing someone else's money.

Imagine you have to run out to work and you're screaming at home, "What's the weather like?"

Looking out the window, you noticed that it's cloudy outside and all you want to know from the answer is whether you should bring an umbrella or not. You are nervously waiting, and this is the answer you get: "It is cloudy now, with clarification, wind speed - eleven meters per second, humidity - eighty-eight percent. Sunset is expected at sixteen forty-nine, and the moon is waning. Oh, yes, the probability of precipitation is ten percent.

From this long text, almost all the information was not needed. And only the last short sentence still explained to you that the umbrella is not needed and it is quite possible to do with a jacket with a hood.

Unfortunately, the people around us often give too much information about anything. They do not take into account the fact that they are wasting someone else's time delaying the presentation of their thoughts.

I'm all for efficiency. Especially at work, where everyone has seven hours strictly devoted to their work. I'm not impressed when an employee hits himself in the chest with the words: "I'm at least an hour late every day!". You have to judge the quality of your work by the results.

Verification often reveals that the performance of such an employee is not higher than that of others. He simply does not have time to do what others do on a working day.

I, therefore, try to save time wherever possible. Later on, I will introduce you to the rules that ultimately optimize time. This rule is one of these. If you can be brief, you have to be brief and not take up your time and that of others.

I could write a whole page of discussions about the fact that time is an irreplaceable resource. And you know what the irony is? I'm going to take some of that resource away from you. But not everyone around you understands that. And their "theft" becomes apparent when nothing is returned.

Before, one of my colleagues could call me in the hallway and say, "Got a minute?"

I tried to be responsive, so I stopped to listen. Only, in the end, a minute would drag on for a quarter of an hour. Although you could do it in sixty seconds. It's just that there are people who like to talk, clarify, ask around.

Now to all those who like to talk at work, I say: "Let's go outside of work hours, and now it's time to do business."

Well, that's the normal answer. But what to do when an employee is very slow in formulating his thoughts about work? What if he discusses work moments for a long time and spends his total time in this way? This is the fourth rule for such cases.

Turn a person around with the words "You've been pulling again..." - that's rude. But it's polite to remind you of the rule. Now I'm just interrupting an employee if he talks long, and please be more specific. If he can't do it right away, I say: "Imagine that you only have five minutes to tell me the most important thing. What would you say to me then?"

I'm not an innovator. Since the middle of the last century, there has been a rule of presentation in the elevator, or elevator pitch, in entrepreneurship. It came into being when startuppers at the time were looking for investors. They ran into a skyscraper elevator with them when they were going about their business. And while the elevator was going and the investors were not busy, start-up entrepreneurs explained the essence and profitability of their business.

Now the rule of presentation in the elevator has spread to all areas of life, where you need to sell your idea. The publishers are waiting for the writer to give them the concept of the book in two sentences. Producers want to know the plot of the script in fifteen seconds.

By and large, any story can fit into several phrases. Any book, film, historical event, religion... Everything. Well, speaking of work situations:

◆ set a task;

◆ to report on the work done;

◆ to remind you of the event;

◆ to present a new project;

◆ to talk about the terms of the deal.

It is difficult to get used to this rule at once. It is generally accepted that all managers are by nature clear and concise. In most cases, this is true, but still, I know enough managers and owners who like to distract from the topic. I also notice that I can repeat myself when I want to give a comprehensive answer.

Here, everything depends on internal censorship. There are work situations where you can't be brief. Sometimes it is necessary to explain, detail, repeat a couple of times, set accents. For example, in the same presentation of the new corporate rule. Yes, it fits into one or two sentences. But to present it to the team and discuss possible objections, you have to invest time.

I advise to distinguish such situations from those where a couple of words are enough. And be sure to teach that to your employees. Again, and again, bring them back to the need to clearly express their thoughts. Teach them to be brief.

Some companies can accomplish hundreds of tasks in an eight-hour working day, while others can accomplish dozens of them at the same time. Some managers concisely explain the point, while others convene ten meetings per day.

And another technique that has become part of my philosophy. Previously I always said that I spend time on work, reading, family, sports... Now I do not spend, and invest, or invest it. It's worth replacing the word, how the same things are perceived in a completely different way. This is the essence of a positive perception of the world, and even such a familiar word change something inside us.

That is why I wish you and your employees to invest time only in effective communication. After all, our working days consist of minutes. And we want to achieve as much as possible during this time! Do we want to achieve as much as possible?

What gives the rule

"Speak briefly and in essence. "Take care of your time and that of others."

◆ Saves manager and employee time.

◆ Learns to formulate thoughts clearly and concisely.

◆ Disciplines and helps distinguish between what is important and what is secondary.

Fifth rule

Give me exactly as many answers as there are questions.

The manager does not ask rhetorical questions.

When you are asked a lot of questions, you should choose the most innocuous from all of them, and then express yourself about it, emotionally expressing and going into a lot of details. You just need to put all the other questions in the background.

From a typical article on how to get away from answering uncomfortable questions.

I'm all for written communication. There'll be a separate rule about it, where I'll detail why the company wins...

from the implementation of this principle. In this chapter, I will talk about how to prevent one situation that could destroy any written negotiations.

The main purpose of written communication in a company is to minimize the negative impact of the human factor. It is not that all people are bad and it is impossible to negotiate with them. It's not at all. It's just that with time each of us forgets details, confuses events, and generally switches to completely new things. Even now you have read this list and have already forgotten what was first on the list.

It's okay, you and I are not robots, and this way of thinking is due to the specifics of our brain. It knows how to filter information and highlight what it needs. You don't have to be a neurobiologist to understand that.

It's very different when we talk about working communication. Written communication is designed to "leave forever" the right information. If one or the other employees suddenly need it, it can be easily restored.

But this principle sometimes does not fully work because of the same selectivity in human thinking. Example: In a task inside a management system, I set three questions for the performer:

1. At what stage is the task?

2. Why didn't you reset the table I asked for?

3. When will the final version be ready?

When an employee sees so many questions from his manager with obvious dissatisfaction, he has one desire: to protect himself as soon as possible. He wants to calm down the dissatisfied manager and in the same task, he assures: "It's all right! The final version will be on Friday".

That's great! And where are the answers to the first two questions? The employee decided that only the last question is essential. The first two are just logical eyeliner. Well, that's not true.

In such cases, I write right in the question: "Answer all the questions!"

Only then the employee answers everything. Such a personal approach to an ordinary employee has a plus - in the future, he will probably answer all the questions in order. The downside is that I have lost my time and God knows how many more times I will lose it in this kind of communication with other employees. Without following this rule, such misunderstandings happen frequently. Employees usually answer one question on the list:

◆ to the easiest;

◆ to the first;

◆ to the last;

◆ to the one, they know the answer to.

That's not how it works. If a manager or a colleague asks consecutive questions, they should be answered accordingly. Otherwise, the whole sense of working communication is lost.

The second part of this rule follows from the first. It says that the manager does not ask rhetorical questions. If this is not emphasized, employees will not understand. I came to this idea after a series of approximately identical correspondence with employees. They looked like this:

- Why are you late? When are you going to drop yesterday's report?

- I'm gonna drop it now.

- And why are you late?

- I won't do it again...

- I didn't ask if you were gonna be late or not. I asked for a reason.

- It's the traffic.

- And what conclusion did you draw?

- I'm leaving the house 20 minutes early tomorrow.

The point of my question about being late was to find out why, not just to show my displeasure with the fact.

But almost no employee answered it immediately and directly.

I and my top managers do not have the time or desire to explain to each employee individually what to answer all the questions and why it is necessary to do so. I'm sure you have more important things to do, too. That is why I have introduced a rule about answers at the corporate level.

And to make the team a little clearer, I gave them advice on how not to make a mistake:

◆ Count the number of question marks in your colleague's or manager's message. Then count the number of your answers. If these numbers match, you did the right thing.

◆ Even simpler: copy the question message and paste your answers one by one under each number. This will make your conversation partner even more comfortable.

This is not a life story. They are just mechanical actions that are worth making the norm in your daily written communications.

The purpose of this rule is not to establish a total dictatorship and control every step of your employees. Its purpose is to teach them how to communicate responsibly in their daily work. If someone asks a question, they probably want an answer. It's important to understand.

So, if you also like order and clarity in the company, I recommend this two-in-one rule. It helped us; it won't let you down!

What gives the rule

"Give exactly as many answers as there are questions. The manager does not ask rhetorical questions."

◆ Helps to save important data.

◆ Disciplines.

◆ Develops a culture of working communication.

◆ Teaches employees to respect each other.

Sixth rule

Comment not on the whole text, but every completed thought.

The incoherent thoughts expressed through coherent speech can indeed easily be deceived and pretended to be the fruit of reason.

In the previous chapter, I wrote that by the number of question marks in a message, the employee can already understand how many answers are expected from him. But it's not just questions that require answers. Often, we write in the statement task. They are followed by dots, but these statements also need comments. So do the questions.

This rule can save working time for whole departments. And at the same time, do not turn the work into chaos. Here's an example from the grey days.

In a luck manager, there is a task where you need to form the conditions of customer service for a new product. Colleagues are discussing their main characteristics. There are many points:

◆ delivery;

◆ warranty;

◆ payment methods;

◆ any undisclosed service to produce "wow effect".

All four items are important for the task. And all of them need to be agreed upon and approved. But for colleagues, the most controversial is the last one. The first three seem to be all standard, but the gift to customers want to discuss properly.

How is the correspondence in the task? The first employee writes: "I offer such a delivery, such a guarantee, such as payment methods and such a promotion.

The next one is connected: "And I suggest to change the action a little: it is better to organize it like this.

Then come the other colleagues, and in the end, all amicably discuss only one position out of four. The first three probably require some improvement, but nobody remembers them anymore. After half a day, they come back: "Guys, so with delivery, warranty, and payment?"

One of the colleagues picks them up: "Yes, about the guarantee..."

And everybody's discussing just one thought again. As a result, an entire department or project team discusses simple enough things all day long. They could have done it in half an hour if they had kept order.

What I feel most sorry for is those colleagues who are added to such a task after a while. This is where the real training for the brain is to understand and structure the whole flow of unrelated thoughts. Yes, you can find quite long texts in standard discussions on tasks. Sometimes they are not structured in any way, but are presented as a continuous "sheet". Here we have a question to the authors of such messages. But even in such difficult situations, employees need to separate from the stream of consciousness of the colleague's individual thoughts and comment on them. This approach solves several questions at once:

◆ Gives a complete picture.

A comment on each thought explains to participants that a comprehensive approach is needed.

◆ Does not irritate colleagues.

If you comment on one thought out of five, the manager has to constantly ask: "What do you think about it? And what do you think about it?" Constant updates only irritate other chat participants. And annoyed colleagues are ineffective colleagues.

◆ Saves time.

It's easier to read everything once than to ask around and give answers.

The same rule also applies to tasks that require feedback on the employee's performance. For example, the designer has attached the developed logo of a new product and two advertising banners to the task. He is waiting for comments on all items. Therefore, the inspector needs to remember the rule that the feedback was effective.

As usual, I have introduced this rule, not on a space. My advice to you: do not bring the situation in communications to a complete mess. The longer it takes, the harder it is to retrain the staff.

In addition to the rule itself, I recommend writing comments on the task. This is a kind of checklist, which shows if you can publish your message:

◆ The message is divided into paragraphs.

◆ Each paragraph is a new idea.

If the message has passed this preliminary control, you can click "Send". When everyone respects the culture of communication, it will be much easier to achieve results.

What gives the rule

"Comment not on the whole text, but every completed thought."

◆ Visual and semantic order in a task or correspondence.

◆ Discipline in communication.

◆ Responsible attitude towards your own words.

Seventh rule

Never be afraid to approach a personal guide and working questions. The doors of any manager are always open for you!

We help people so that they, in turn, help us. In this way, our services are reduced to the benefits we provide to ourselves in the future.

François de La Rochefoucauld.

One day an employee came to me and told me he was going to quit. I was surprised: as long as I remember, this man was good at his job and loyal to the company. Of course, I wanted to know the reason. And that's what I heard:

"I've been working for a year now and I've been doing the same tasks all the time. I have to develop, and here I can't do it. So, I found another company that wants to meet me."

That answer stunned me. Why didn't a colleague keep quiet for a year? His situation can't even be called a problem. As soon as he voiced it, I had several options in mind to solve it:

◆ to propose a new position;

◆ add new areas of responsibility;

◆ to ask him to develop a new direction.

If he had approached earlier, when he first discovered this feeling of "fermenting in a circle", we would have solved this issue together. And we would do it in a mutually beneficial way: the employee would achieve his goals with the help of the company, and the company - with the help of the employee.

Instead, he has come to what he has already agreed with his new employer. His issue could have been resolved much earlier without problems. So, I asked him:

- Why didn't you come sooner?

- I didn't think it was possible?

At that moment I realized that the team members are efficient and effective when they feel comfortable. Not only physically, but also psychologically. It's not enough for people just to have soft chairs and a social package. They need even more responsiveness and ponies.

I have become more attentive to watching the staff. It turned out that some people walk around the office gloomy. They were immersed in their thoughts and not thinking about work. When I asked what happened to them, it turned out that one of them in the morning on the bus stole a wallet, another one is now sick.

People are the company's greatest asset. Their condition and mood have a significant impact on their effectiveness. If you don't believe me, believe the research results. Scientists have found that happy employees work twelve percent more productively than unhappy people. They are also thirty-one percent more efficient, thirty-seven percent more successful at selling, their customers are twenty-two percent more satisfied, they are thirty percent healthier and three times more likely to find creative solutions.

Impressive, isn't it? That's why large companies - Zappos, Microsoft, Ebay, Google, Toyota - have opened "happiness departments" and introduced a new position of Chief Happiness Officer, or "general manager of happiness". Such CHO, or HR2.0, monitors and manages employees' emotional state.

It doesn't mean that we all have to open "happiness departments" in our companies immediately. It is enough to realize the correlation between the emotional background of an employee and the results of his activity. This alone will allow us to understand how to improve our HR department and what indicators to expect from it.

In my companies, we practice the HR tool "individual conversation". The task of the conversation is to determine the level of the employee's satisfaction with the company and to increase it as much as possible.

You can see an example of questions for an individual conversation here.

In my experience, there is a good example that will explain to you the importance of this method.

During the next individual conversation, I asked the employee a question on duty, offering to evaluate their satisfaction with the company on a ten-point scale.

This person has never opposed the company's policy and I counted on his appreciation. But he was awarded six points.

When I started to find out why that was the number, something came out that I did not expect.

A few months ago, his mother went to the hospital. When he ran out of money, he went to his direct supervisor to ask for a loan. He said no, and the employee was offended by the whole company.

As I then found out, the employee did not explain to his top manager why he needed such a large sum of money. Of course, he'd have been helped out. But there was a misunderstanding that led to a decrease in this person's loyalty to the company as a whole.

This disloyalty was reflected in the employee's performance. He began to perform tasks of a lower quality. He had only one thought in his head: "If the company is not ready to give me more, why should I give it something?".

Of course, I offered to lend him the necessary amount of money and made it clear that if he was refused by his immediate superior, he could safely go to a superior. This conversation immediately bore fruit: the efficiency and quality of this worker's work as a whole has increased noticeably.

It's the same with working questions. A man can fight for a week on one task and secretly hate everyone. He will have an outrage: "Why isn't anyone helping me? Still, they see me suffering!"

Unfortunately, we almost always focus on ourselves and rarely notice other people's feelings. Or we notice when ordinary experiences have already grown into open aggression. Later, I opened a full-fledged HR department, whose task is to monitor and prevent such situations in time.

But the first thing I did was to introduce a rule that any employee can approach the management on personal and working issues. I would not have introduced it if it was not important for me to keep good employees.

Now any member of my team can discuss their condition at least with their immediate supervisor. And here as well as in the rational suggestion system: if one top is not withdrawn, the employee has the right to move up until he reaches the owner.

Usually, the managers I tell about this rule have the fear: "What if everyone starts complaining and deliberately seeks benefit from our responsiveness?

That's what I've taken into account too. Managers do not rush to solve an employee's problem immediately. They still remind us that the responsibility remains with him. So, after they voice the problem, they ask, "How could you solve it?" They continue to look at the adequacy of the sentence. If the employee says really good things and asks for a new interesting task, to replace the broken computer, it can be taken to work.

But if the employee complains that his motivation and efficiency are decreasing because he is not picked up by a taxi every morning, this can be missed. The exception is when an employee breaks his leg and has a real difficulty moving around. But then you can offer him to work remotely.

There is always a way out. The main thing is to check the complaints of employees for adequacy and, if necessary, return them to respond.

Now one of my companies - "World of Libra" - employs more than a hundred people. Of course, not all of them have problems every day, but they still want to get attention. They are all the more aware of this rule. And the worst thing about the rule is when it is, but it doesn't work. We'll talk about it at the end of the book, and in the meantime, I'll tell you what we came up with.

For each member of the team to get the promised attention, we and the HR-department regularly hold individual conversations with employees, and we also came up with such a "chip" as a mailbox "Talk to the owner". I visit the office of this company four hours a week because no more is required of me there. It is already systematized enough to work successfully without the owner.

Thanks to this mail, I stay in touch with my team. And although I am not in the office with them, I can still monitor the psychological state of the team - "the overall temperature in the hospital". Plus, I'm always in close contact with the HR department.

Think about how hard it is for you to part with a really good employee. If you are not attached to a team and it is important for you to close your area of responsibility, you may not need this rule. I'm not saying that your approach is wrong. In a competitive market, this is a normal situation. All the more reason to make your business so that your employees become indispensable.

But whatever team policy you pursue, I still advise you to treat people as a very valuable resource. When they are doing well, they take it over to their tasks and close them down many times more effectively.

Which gives the rule.

"Never be afraid to approach the manual on personal and business matters. The doors of any manager are always open to you!"

◆ Improves team efficiency.

◆ Improves the microclimate.

◆ It allows the manager to keep his hand on the pulse and track his dissatisfaction with the company in time.

◆ Prevents conflict and disloyalty to the company.

◆ Gives employees a sense of security.

Eighth rule

Answers "No time" or "I forgot" mean wrong prioritization and are no excuse.

Ninety-nine percent of all failures are from people who have a habit of making excuses.

George Washington.

As you have noticed, this rule echoes the third: "Not sure - do not promise. "If you promise, do it! It's all about the responsibility of the employees and whether they feel...

part of the workflow.

And yet this rule is a little different. Unlike the third one, it is aimed not so much at performance as at planning. Although these things are connected and always go side by side, in this chapter I will focus on effective time management.

I am convinced that there are no impossible tasks. There is only wrong planning. So, when an employee says, "I forgot" or "There was no time" on a deadline day, I hear:

"I can't plan my time."

Forgetting a task is natural. We can hold on to five, eight things at a time. Not only workers but also personal ones. While we are doing the task, our brain is already thinking about where to go for lunch and what to order this time.

When I ask employees to plan time, I don't mean to remember everything. On the contrary! I'm asking you to shift this case to technology. And it's on them, not in notebooks and notes. At the very beginning of our company, in the harsh "zero", my team and I did not yet know about online calendars and shuffle managers. That's why we had such a special "blue book" - a handheld prototype of an online calendar. It was a big notebook that we had sorted out for some functionality. In this book, we tried to plan all our tasks and activities. But what did we do?

◆ Some things were superimposed on others.

◆ There was some confusion.

◆ Tasks were lost.

In such a medieval approach it was not surprising to hear from someone the sacramental phrase: "I forgot".

Because a bad system + limited memory capacity = expired tasks and workflow failure.

Now everything is different. I introduced the rule that one should plan one's time and not put colleagues and supervisors before the fact: "I forgot" - when everyone expected that this work would be done.

However, you have to agree, it would be unfair to require the team to be executive and not to give it all the resources. I, therefore, ask managers and all employees to manage themselves. In doing so, I have explained how to do it and with what power.

These items have now become mandatory rules for our corporate planning. Take a look at them. I hope they will be useful to you and guide your team.

Plan online.

I start with this point because everyone else is holding on to it. And I insist: it is the online planning that suits our crazy workload. My team and I use the Google Calendar. These are its main advantages:

◆ it's easy to get all the information you need about your holiday into it.

◆ tasks are easy to move.

◆ they don't get lost.

◆ it's visible all week, and you can estimate your load in seconds.

It also makes it easier for employees to interact:

◆ colleagues can access each other's calendars (for example, the whole department can see the manager's chart).

◆ the manager quickly assesses the workload of his subordinates and assigns tasks correctly.

◆ the calendar of all meeting rooms in the office allows employees to book them quickly.

The online calendar has many more advantages. Go to it, if you're not already there, and poach the same assistant or secretary. When you feel all its convenience, you can implement rules for the whole team.

Enter the tasks in a certain order.

First, it is worth adding those that are repeated day by day or with another regular sequence: lunches, gliders, etc. Then - cases with a specific timing: meetings, negotiations, interviews.

All remaining tasks should be entered according to their timing and priorities. That's what we're talking about below.

Take into account the priority of tasks

The best tool for determining the priority of a task is the Eisenhower Matrix. You probably know about it. It is important that your employees also use it if you want to implement a complete planning.

All employees' priorities are determined by their managers. Employees also need to understand that the priority of tasks changes over time: from an urgent and important task to an urgent and important one. This needs to be monitored.

Keep track of deadlines

The importance of establishing clear deadlines for each task will be addressed by a separate rule ahead. But already here I can emphasize an important point. To prevent the same "no time", the task should not be stuck to the deadline. Or at least try not to do so, if the schedule allows. Otherwise, the manager will get a "raw" result, and there will be no time to finalize it.

Leave time for unplanned tasks

What does the employee's answer "There was no time" mean? It means that he didn't find time between tasks that followed one another. But this would not have happened if he had left time in his calendar for sudden tasks.

I ask all my employees to do the following: to allocate an hour or two per day to such cases. This time must be allocated and "Urgent Affairs" signed. If this is not done, it will be difficult for the employee to navigate in a busy schedule.

Break down complex tasks.

Or "eat an elephant in pieces." This means that you have to write one large-scale task for many small subtasks. It is easier to plan them over time and distribute them among employees. The best helpers are the two tools: the mental maps and the Gantt chart.

Besides online planning, there is another cool tool - control points. For an employee not to put the team in front of a sad fact already on the last day, the manager or a special person can check it during the whole term. This must be done on certain dates, which are agreed in advance between the employee and the manager.

An important point: During the checkpoint, the employee himself must show the manager the current situation, not vice versa! The responsibility lies with the employee. If he does not report at the appointed time, the manager has the right to ask himself. But already after the control point, not before.

This is the minimum time management knowledge that can bear fruit. You just have to apply them. At first, it was not easy for me to get used to the Google Calendar. But it's not that it's uncomfortable. The only inconvenience was getting used to the new one. You have to admit, it's always hard at first.

But believe me: after a couple of weeks, you cannot live without quality planning. When I saw it, I shouldn't have brought it to the team anymore.

I don't think that time management is magic, and as soon as a person registers in the online calendar, he develops an anomaly and he immediately, automatically, starts to do more than before. Of course not. A calendar is first and foremost an opportunity to look at your tasks over time. It's one thing to write them out on a sheet. And quite another thing is to look at how many hours they take in a real day.

Not all people by nature are administrators. And employees first need to address their time management. I wish you wouldn't have to hear "No time" and "I forgot" from your wards. Let these phrases stay in the past and effective planning appears in the present!

What gives the rule

"No time" or "I forgot" means wrong prioritization and is no excuse."

◆ Does not allow employees to use a childish "excuse".

◆ Teaches the team to plan their time and set priorities.

◆ It frees the mind from having to keep things in your head and puts them on the shoulders of technology.

◆ It makes the company more efficient through a more cohesive process.

Ninth rule

If you think that you are ready to take on new responsibilities, to develop, to move up the career ladder - tell your manager and HR-specialist.

Your development and motivation to achieve your goals are important to your management.

If you decide to help a suffering person, do so only based on his or her merits, his or her efforts to cope with his or her distress, his or her reasonableness, or on the basis that he or she has suffered unfairly. Then help will remain a bargain - exchange your help for his virtue. But to help a person without virtues, to help only because he suffers, to help simply because as arguments he puts forward his shortcomings, his needs - is like giving up his values for nothing.

Ayn Rand "Atlante has straightened his shoulders."

This rule, like everyone else, was not born of a fairytale state of affairs. But as we've learned before, stability is not so good. That's why I'm glad there's a breakdown in the workplace...

The process has led to the creation of effective rules.

One day our company was relieved of a management position and I approved an employee for it. I did not regret my choice, but something else happened. I noticed that another employee, who until recently was a colleague of the new top, is dissatisfied with the situation. And he expresses his dissatisfaction with the claims to the whole company: he does not agree with the innovations, is rude, does not want to perform his duties.

I must say that this man has always been a good employee, and this behavior was immediately noticeable. Naturally, the efficiency of his work has decreased. In a personal conversation, he explained the reason for his demotivation:

- I have been working here for a long time, always supporting the company, developing and showing good results in my work. Why did you not appoint me as a manager?

- Why didn't you tell your direct supervisor or me what you wanted to do?

- I thought it was clear enough!

As it turns out, no. Let me tell you more: even with a perfectly developed corporate culture and a system HR department, the management is not always able to understand the intentions of each employee. What he is silent about is his secret.

So, I understood that it is time to introduce another rule and tell people: "Please, initiate such conversations first! The company may meet you, but you're the first step!"

Employees can work hard and show great results. Of course, management notices this and tries to encourage it in some way. But when a specialist reaches the limit of professional development and does not hint at a desire to change his position, the company can leave everything in place.

The management can consider the silence of even the highest-class employee as: "This person is a good performer. He wants to achieve excellence in his field, and he has no leadership ambition. Let's leave him in a comfortable environment if he likes it so much.

Many employees think that in the office of each top and key employee there are twenty monitors on which they track the behavior of each one and put the markers opposite the scale.

"Ready for promotion." Not at all. Managers notice those who want to be seen for themselves.

I used to think it was obvious. Especially, I put people in management positions who were still speaking about their goals in the interview. It seemed to me that the mechanism was already working well. Everyone who wants to talk about their ambitions.

But no. Just as capable, but more humble people lack some kind of push. And the general corporate rule was that push. It tells employees: "You can grow. Whether you want to take the initiative or not is your choice. But you're not going to say for sure, "I didn't know."

Such transparency of processes is a necessity for any company. It excludes all kinds of gossip, rumors, and chatter in the smoke.

The career ladder's been sorted out. What else is there to control this rule? Development isn't just about vertical growth. Employees can grow above themselves by remaining in the same position or moving linearly. Here are some ways:

◆ get new areas of responsibility in your field.

◆ to develop in a new profession, in a new position within the same company.

◆ to acquire new knowledge to do his or her job even better.

If you as a manager are willing to provide such opportunities to your team, let them know directly.

Once, I suggested for two weeks that a new PR-manager goes on a good training course. He refused all the time. As it turned out, he thought I was obliging him to pay for the training from my pocket. Only you make the rules. I hope we agree with you that people are the most valuable resource of the company and they need to be developed. New knowledge is not always available for free. Training programs, online courses, new editions of business literature - all this almost always for a fee. If you can ensure your employees and pay for them in the following way give them new knowledge, do it.

You don't have to pay the whole amount. It is possible to divide the costs in a "fifty to fifty" ratio or to agree on a system of working out. When the owner introduces a rule.

"Be sure to develop", it must provide the necessary resources for the staff. Most often in cash.

I also noticed that about every two years a person subconsciously expects change. If he or she has been standing still for more than a year, he or she may become disappointed. Employees do not always realize and track this feeling within themselves, but they may experience it.

Therefore, HR professionals or managers need to know how long each employee has been in their position.

When the deadline approaches two years, all receptors must be turned on and the behavior of this person monitored closely.

It is not necessary to conduct a detective surveillance. You can simply initiate a personal conversation with the employee and find out what he wants. Believe me: in two years any developing employee has already formed enough goals in his head. Before moving on to the next rule, I want to remind you of a business axiom: the company is moving at the speed of the weakest top manager; the department is developing at the speed of the weakest employee. I hope that you understand the importance of training and developing your team. This is first and foremost beneficial for the owner. When I realized it and introduced the corresponding rule, things went better. It's true!

What gives the rule

"If you think you're ready to take on new responsibilities, develop, move up the career ladder," tell your manager and HR specialist.

Your development and motivation to achieve your goals is important to your management.

◆ Enhancement mechanism transparency.

◆ Psychological comfort of employees: everyone is happy to feel in their place. Happy employees are efficient employees.

◆ Awareness among all team members that the responsibility for their development lies with them.

◆ Increasing employees' initiative.

Tenth rule

Wrongly executed task - unfulfilled task!

Incorrectly completed task - a task that has not been completed in time!

Not completely fulfilled task - unfulfilled task!

I wasn't mad at them for being late. So why would they be mad at me for not waiting for them?

Mario Puso.

"Fools are dying."

Each owner and manager choose his management policy. Some achieve results from the staff, through incentives, others through fines. Some give a second chance, others fire. But this rule is universal: it is suitable for any company, no matter what values its owner is guided by. I will explain why.

For a long time, I have noticed that some employees have a purely school belief: the main thing is effort. Probably in every school were especially angry teachers who gave good marks out of pity or sympathy. Those who actively used it carried this delusion through life right to his workplace.

But the fact is that a job is not a school or a university. At work, there are clear conditions for cooperation. The company is obliged to pay a person a salary. But to get it, a person must produce results. Next, I will devote a separate chapter on how to train employees to focus on the result. In the meantime, let's get to the bottom of this rule.

Originally the new rule sounded like: "Wrongly executed task - unfulfilled task". Thus, I decided to insure myself and my top managers from wasting time. And time was spent managers had to check the tasks, point out errors, and return the tasks with explanations, what exactly they were not satisfied with.

A carelessly executed task slows down the workflow one way or another. But here the difficulty arose. It turned out that this sentence alone does not solve the problem. The word "wrong" was not quite clear. And then the rule itself came up with all the language you see above.

If you combine all the pieces of the big rule into one, you get the following: "Wrongly executed task - task whose result does not meet the original requirements".

There is no room for excuses in the style of "But I tried". No matter how close an employee gets to a hundred percent, he cannot defend himself if he has not completed the task in full. He can say that he has completed a part of the task, and this will be true. But the truth is also that he was not asked to complete a part of the task, but to complete the whole task.

Let's say that you instructed your assistant to buy you a plane ticket. And he got so worked up that he started looking for it when all the seats onboard were already occupied by more prudent passengers.

Or he had already entered the site and even selected the necessary flight, but then he was distracted by another task, and he completely forgot about your ticket!

Or maybe he ignored your request to find a connecting flight to Istanbul and chose another one. He liked that transplant better. And it doesn't matter that it was important for you to stay in the city where you planned the meeting.

All the situations that I have just listed are examples of tasks that have not been properly carried out, i.e. not completed. Yes, your assistant has spent his time on them and yours. Yeah, he was doing the right thing for a while. But what does it matter if you didn't end up on your plane? And if you did, it wasn't on the flight you were originally planning.

Delayed time, incompleteness, wrong sequence of actions - all these are reasons to consider the task unfulfilled. Even if the employee has spent several working hours on it, this does not justify him.

I rarely see companies where absolutely every employee thinks about the size of the whole company. Rather, the opposite is true: ordinary team members focus on their work and consider it the most important.

Therefore, when a person does a task wrong for one reason or another, he has a lot of arguments to justify it. And the truth is: he had ten other tasks in addition to yours, and he was distracted.

Previously, I tried to get into the position of every such employee. Now I realize that's not quite right. I realized that it simply made no sense to deal with each individual, finding out what had prevented him from completing the task properly. But it's in my power as a manager to give my team the tools to make it easier for employees to work.

Planning, written communication, flexible schedule, comfortable office - these and other conveniences allow the team to focus on their work. In return, I put forward my condition: a task counts when it is completed according to the original requirements. In any other case, it is considered not fulfilled at all.

There are often people in teams who systematically make the same mistakes. They still have a schoolboy inside who requires special treatment or just leniency. They still think that they can do a couple of tasks from the huge homework, and the rest of the responsibility they will be relieved of a note from their mother.

Sometimes the team needs to explain that it's impossible to jump ninety-eight percent. A hundred percent is the minimum that is possible at work. Even if it's half a percent lower, it won't work anymore. Partially, even if of high quality, the completed task has no value for the company.

It is extremely important to explain these things to your employees. Once and for all. Otherwise, it will be necessary to constantly waste time on unnecessary conversations, which prolong the already overdue process.

I advise you to print this rule separately and hang it in the form of a poster in the most prominent place in the office. People should remember what you expect from them. They need to know what their salary and position in the company depend on.

In my team, this rule has improved performance. Yes, there are still violations: somebody slips deadlines, somebody performs only part of the task, somebody ignores the sequence of actions. But now all this is not regarded as an unfortunate accident, but as a violation of a rule known to all, and the violator understands why his efforts were not counted.

Put specificity in the relationship between the delegator and the executor. It is better to let everyone know their role in the task than to break the business process and let the whole team down.

What gives the rule

"Wrongly executed job - wrongly executed job! Incorrectly completed task - task not completed! Incomplete job - unfulfilled job. "An agreed task, performed by uncoordinated actions, is an unfulfilled task!"

◆ It does not allow employees to make childish excuses.

◆ Teaches the team to focus on the result.

◆ Makes the wards more attentive to the important details of the tasks.

◆ Develops responsibility for their contribution to the overall process.

Eleventh rule

Tasks are accepted only in written form.

If an assignment is given orally, duplicate it in writing.

*An oral agreement is not worth the paper on which it is written. ***

Samuel Goldwyn

*The phrase belongs to Samuel Goldwyn, one of Hollywood's most successful producers and co-founder of Metro-Goldwyn- Mayer with the famous growling lion on his logo. Ironically, many employees have remembered Goldwyn as a stingy manager. He promised them prizes and bonuses every time a new carina was successful. The films did indeed become successful, but the producer did not keep his verbal promises.

A few years ago, one of our managers instructed his new assistant to negotiate with Chinese suppliers for the next batch of weighing equipment. This is a standard task for Mir Weighing. The assistant had all the conditions: a good level of English, any messengers and enough time to deadline.

She called and made a deal. It seems like a happy ending. But soon it turned out that the suppliers had not kept some of their promises and were out of sight. A week later, they answered the calls, but their words didn't bode well:

- What kind of arrangements? We don't know what you mean. We didn't make any promises!

What did the leader do? He reminded his assistant about the rule:

- Only negotiate in writing, and any messages with questions are supported by screenshots of previous correspondence.

Did the suppliers fail after that? Of course, they did. The corporate rule can in no way affect people who do not work within the company. However, it has allowed us to argue for general agreements in a reasonable manner:

- Here are your words, see for yourself.

When the assistant was promoted to sales manager, she was most pleased that she would no longer have to communicate with suppliers from China. She remembers them as very complicated people. But is that it?

In Chapter Four, I promised to tell you in detail why I believe it is vital to introduce written communication in the company. I think this example, better than any explanation, supports my point of view.

It's not about the difficulties of translation. I am sure that everyone will have at least one example of how agreements were broken. Both sides blamed someone else's dishonesty or bad memory, although the real reason is much more prosaic. Very often misunderstandings with contractors lie in oral communication.

Yes, many companies have long since moved exclusively to written negotiations with external partners. But for some reason, not everyone has implemented this principle within their business. But what's the difference? Colleagues promise something to each other in the same way, make commitments, share responsibility.

I have introduced written communication for over eight years and now I see that this step has become one of the most important in the systematization of business.

What does it take to implement the rule? Ideally, a management system in which all employees work. It also includes messengers, where your working chats are created.

Step away from the topic a little bit and I will focus on the management system. If it is already implemented in your company, you will agree with me. For me, it is a prerequisite for the effective functioning of the company. The system gives you several key opportunities:

◆ to control all tasks simultaneously.

◆ to distribute responsibility.

◆ to save the details of each task.

◆ to keep track of the deadlines.

◆ write down the expected result.

Messenger is already an auxiliary tool, which is more suitable for informal communication, some clarifications, or just for work jokes. It is not intended to be a complete tool for tasks there. And it is not only about limited functionality, where even the deadline cannot be set. Messengers are simply unreliable. Don't forget that it's easy to lose your message history.

So, for the full work of any company you need a sales manager. And why do you need written communication? To have a sales manager perform the functions I listed above. To discuss tasks only in writing is a mandatory condition that ensures the effectiveness of the whole idea.

Written task management benefits the sleeper in many ways.

Judge for yourself.

The details are preserved.

In the first half-hour after accepting the task, the employee still remembers all the details. After a month, he no longer remembers that such a task was at all. The habit of saving everything in electronic form allows all old and new participants to remember the conditions of the task.

Additional agreement

If one employee assigned a task to another orally, the performer must duplicate the task in writing. With this approach, the delegator looks at the assignment once more and confirms that everything is correct. And if the performer has made a mistake, the delegator can correct it immediately before the work has begun.

Clear timeframe

You can set the deadline for the task. In this way, the person in charge will complete everything on time.

Control Points

Thanks to the electronic fixation, the delegator can always check the intermediate results to correct them if necessary. For this purpose, the control points are agreed upon by the colleagues in the task, and on the appointed dates, the contractor provides his work.

The responsibility lies with one person.

The task manager function assumes only one person responsible for the task. Yes, there can be many performers, but there is one person responsible for each zone. This means that the manager always knows who to contact if something has to be reworked.

Saving time.

Each employee has access to the task force during the whole working hours. As soon as one colleague has set a task to another, the performer will see it and be able to plan it immediately. If you look for a colleague throughout the office, the process takes place.

Additional materials

You can upload any materials on the topic: documentations, links, images, videos, presentations. In correspondence, all this would be confused.

Training an employee to tasks that have already been performed.

Every new employee must undergo a process of adaptation. They are explained how their work processes are carried out, how their daily tasks should be carried out. This process is considerably reduced if a newcomer is added to the task of his predecessor or a person in a similar position. He would sooner understand what other colleagues would explain to him orally for a long time.

Access to information

There are situations when a manager negotiates with an external partner and then quits. And the main question for the management is: what did he do at all? If such an employee did not reflect the results in the tasks, it is impossible to know.

The main condition for the written communication to justify itself is to follow the rule 100%. No more half-measures! If you decided to implement rule number eleven, its implementation should be monitored, and employees should be disciplined.

When companies implement this rule, they often encounter misunderstanding and sabotage from the team. Patience is needed here, as with any other innovation.

I used to implement this rule for the first time, too, and not everyone was happy with it. Some employees could not believe that they would have to reduce meetings and that tasks no longer needed to be discussed for several hours. But in the end, everybody got so used to it that now they can't imagine the workflow any differently. Even when employees discuss new tasks orally, they still duplicate the results of their communication in writing. Of course, they don't write down the whole conversation, but at least they reflect the essence of it.

In this book, written communication is just one of the rules. It is the foundation of a system company. If you want to build a large scalable company, implement this rule! I wouldn't include it in the book if it wasn't effective. How much patience it requires at first proves its fundamentality? Go ahead, I believe in you!

What gives the rule

"Tasks are only accepted in writing. If an assignment is given orally, duplicate it in writing."

◆ Converts the terms of each task into a contract that cannot be broken.

◆ Excludes group responsibility for the task or transfer of responsibility.

◆ Eliminates group responsibility for the task or assignment of responsibility.

◆ Enables management to control all actions of employees within the task.

Twelfth rule

Performed the task - make sure that the manager is familiar with the result.

In teamwork silence is not gold, silence is death.

Marc Sanborn.

Let's imagine a trivial situation: you asked your assistant to make tea. Tell me when you think the task is done when the helper pours boiling water in a cup or when he'll put a cap on your table saying, "Here's your tea"?

I'm for option two. And I'm sure you are, too, because the responsibility for the task is always with the performer. But most of the staff understands responsibility only to fulfill the conditions of the task. Few people consider themselves obliged to notify their manager about the result.

Not only some specialists, but also their managers do not realize this. This is where the problems come from:

◆ managers do not receive the task in time.

◆ employees are demotivated because they don't consider themselves guilty, because they have done their job.

◆ managers are dissatisfied with their clients because they entrusted them with the task but did not get the result in time.

Question: who is to blame in such situations? The answer is impossible because nobody agreed on anything from the very beginning. Both sides were waiting for something from each other: the manager - that the employee will let him know about the completed task, the employee - that the manager will evaluate his work.

The example of tea is simple. Of course, no one would die if the tea cooled down. But what happens if the employee completes some serious task and does not notify the manager about the result? He won't say where he downloaded the presentation to negotiate with his partners, he won't remember that he printed the document for inspection.

A staff member does not always understand that his process is just an inter-office process in a chain. And if the supervisor does not approve his work in time, the next specialist will not get to the task in the planned time.

Therefore, to protect myself and my top managers, I have introduced a rule that the task is considered completed at the moment when the manager received it in his hands or looked through it in a lucky manager.

Someone will consider this rule unnecessary and even unfair: why should the employee do extra work instead of the manager? I agree, he should not do unnecessary work, but this is not the case. We are talking about responsibility and how to bring it up in employees. We are talking about how to make the work process more efficient. All this is impossible if every manager will be watching other people's deadlines and who should do what for him.

To introduce the rule without misunderstanding, it is important to explain to the team that this is not the beginning of a dictatorship, but only one more step in any task for which the specialist is responsible as a performer. Any employee whose work has not been checked in time will have two hands in favor.

Another important goal of this rule is to teach employees to see the true result of their actions. When a sales manager sends several companies a commercial offer, he mechanically sends letters with a file inside. For him, on the Send button, the task ends. But as soon as our twelfth rule is implemented in the company, the manager realizes that at the moment of sending nothing is over.

The employee of the department of sales will execute a task with commercial offers when the addressee notifies it that has familiarized itself with the document. Sometimes the manager himself needs to call the recipient and make sure that the document has been received. In a problem feedback is important: to work in anything - not the most effective approach.

I have noticed that thanks to this rule, they began to appreciate their work more. They do not want their manager not to understand how much effort they have put into it. The colleagues realized that it is in their interest to notify the managers that they have done everything and are waiting for feedback.

Inform your team: the task is considered completed only if the manager has found out about the result. When this rule becomes an axiom, everyone wins!

What gives the rule

"Do the job, make sure the manager is familiar with the result."

◆ Releases managers from having to keep track of deadlines for implementers.

◆ It helps professionals understand the purpose of their actions.

◆ Gives employees the timely feedback they need for their professional development.

◆ Eliminates the need to enquire, which saves overall working time.

Thirteenth rule

Each task must have a set deadline and an end goal!

Didn't the manager say anything? Be sure to specify it yourself!

It's hard to answer for yourself because you don't know who to ask.

Sync by honeybunny

In my training speeches, I ask the audience:

- Raise your hand if you consider the deadline and the end goal as important criteria in the task.

The absolute majority raises their hands. Then I ask the audience to do the following:

- Now raise your hand if you sound them every time you give an employee a task.

Twenty percent is left of the full hand room. That is only one-fifth of the audience. That's not some miserable error of a couple of percent. It's an obvious bias, behind which there's a serious problem.

All leaders are aware of the importance of these two components of the task - term, and goal. Moreover, all managers expect from their team a completely definite result. But the problem is that they omit these moments when delegating the task because they consider the obvious.

What does it work out? Almost all top executives and managers want their employees to accomplish the tasks according to their original goal and in time, and even better before the deadline. However, they talk about it because "it is still clear". Employees receive a task without precise coordinates and are not specified either. They think this way: "If the manager has not voiced such important things, it is not crucial for him/her when I will give up the task and in what form. I will decide for myself".

It turns out that both sides understand that it is necessary to proceed from the term and the goal of the task. But since nobody insisted on it and did not even say it, the question closes by itself.

Sometimes the company becomes more effective not at the expense of any revolutionary ideas. Sometimes it is enough to realize something simple for the situation to change dramatically. The rule of purpose and timing is just from this opera.

You probably think it's strange to chew up an entire chapter of obvious things. Purpose and timing - what's not clear about that? But let me ask you: have you ever found yourself in a situation where you have received from an employee not what you expected?

It's happened to me, more than once. I once had my assistant buy me two tickets to a concert. On the appointed day, I asked her to give them to me. And I got an A4 sheet with printed e-tickets. It was okay, but I was planning on carrying them as a gift. So, on my day off, my assistant had to break down and go to the ticket office to exchange the printout for a more presentable version.

And then one day I asked the employee to make a presentation for my speech. I did not name the date, because the whole team was already working on its preparation. As a result, I did not receive a ready presentation on time because the employee did not understand me.

I have many more such stories, and all of them confirm one idea: the importance of stipulating the deadline and the goal - they must be talked to the manager or ask the performer. Always. Otherwise, you do not set a goal, but only express your vague wish, which is not particularly important now.

I call such ghostly tasks "wishful thinking". They are enough in everyone's life. For years people are going to run in the morning, learn English, travel all over Europe. But these desires remain desires because they are not accompanied by a specific time frame and final goal.

They migrate year after year until one realizes that the moment for their fulfillment is missed.

I suggest that you do not shift this approach to work. For me, the solution is this rule. Now each of my company executives tries to specify a goal and a deadline for any task at once. But even if he forgets about it in a hurry, the employees ask for it themselves. This is the rule. And the team members know that for an unsatisfactory result they will be asked anyway, and all will be rebuked for mistaking the task.

Inform the employees that they have no right to take on the task until such elementary things as the goal and the deadline are clear. Once they have learned this, they will receive comprehensive information even at the zero stage when they are given the task.

You now have in your hands a book on how to make your company effective and how to improve its corporate culture. If that's your wish, turn it into a task - just add a deadline and an end goal. Once you do this, you will have a real motivation to implement the new rules. You will understand why this is necessary. I believe in you, and I wait for the next chapter.

What gives the rule

"Each task must have a deadline and an end goal! Didn't the manager say anything? Make sure you check it out!"

◆ It gives the team a full understanding of the task and its role in solving it.

◆ Prevents possible errors as a result.

◆ Allows a constructive discussion of the result rather than wasting time on finding out where things went wrong.

Fourteenth rule

Only one person can be responsible for a task! Group responsibility is group irresponsibility.

I have a trick that I sometimes use to check with potential executives to see if they're ready for...whine position. For this purpose, I instruct them to take on a project or a major task. In this way, I determine whether a person can control other employees and take responsibility for their results.

For a top manager, this is an inherent feature, but is it only for him? Every employee has to be responsible for the result he or she produces. It doesn't matter how impressive the result is. The office manager has to be sure which wipes he ordered. And the sales manager must be clear about how much profit his wards have brought.

Do you agree with me? If so, let's go straight to the rule. It will be useful to you if you at least once did not know with whom to ask the result of the task. It happens quite often, for example, if:

◆ two or more people are responsible for the same process;

◆ in case of an error or failure, one employee shifts the responsibility to another;

◆ the person who made the mistake is not announced at all.

In any of these situations, the whole process breaks down. Instead of getting the result, the manager has to play Sherlock Holmes. He finds out who was involved in the task, where it all began, and in what direction the process moved. And so, step by step, from employee to employee, until one of them confesses.

It takes a huge amount of time. And the worst part is that such actions are not at all what the manager should do. If he dedicates so much time to operational things, he will not have enough time to perform his tasks.

On the other hand, it is precisely these malfunctions that allow you to see the problem and understand what exactly needs to be improved. In this case, the problem is a group responsibility. I have long understood that this notion in itself is controversial. There is no such thing as group responsibility; there is only group irresponsibility. Only one person should be responsible for one process. One person should also be responsible for a complex and multistage project. How will they interact? It is simple. For employees to complete a complex task, two conditions are needed:

1) an employee responsible for the whole task, who will play the role of distributor and moderator in it;

2) specialists, each of whom will close their area of responsibility according to their skills.

The main moderator employee does not even have to be the performer of one of the pieces of a big task. His mission is in another one:

◆ to distribute subtasks among specialists;

◆ set each term;

◆ to make sure that each performer submits his or her job front in time;

◆ to check if the results meet the original requirements;

◆ provide the final result to the manager.

In such a case, it is important to understand the following: the task moderator is responsible for all processes and all subtotals produced by the specialists. Even if the task moderator has instructed the copywriter to write the article and has only approved it, it is the task moderator who will be responsible to the manager for the quality of this article. And so, in all subtasks and processes.

Not every employee can handle such a task. That's why not every employee is a top manager. To lead other people, you need to have internal strength. And it's not about yelling at the people in charge and making them fear. The power of a manager is to properly distribute responsibility and bring in a team of proven experts.

I will talk about leadership and leadership skills, but for now, I just want to emphasize that group responsibility is a myth. Yes, you can assign a project to a department, but in this case, the head of the department himself will appoint those responsible for each subtask. The main thing is to remember the principle: the person responsible for the task is always one person, and there can be many performers. And each performer must be responsible for his or her part of the work.

The manager or manager who assigned the task to the responsible person must enter the game at the very end. All that is required of him is to come and accept the ready result. He or she does not need to find out exactly where the chain of actions is broken. He does not need to look for the guilty and double-check the result of each.

Sometimes it is very important to go through this period of uncertainty and haphazardness to understand what the company needs.

Developing responsibility in a team is not as easy as it seems. But it is possible. And the prize for the effort is a working mechanism, where all the tasks are performed with high quality and in time. If you aspire to it, pay attention to rule number fourteen!

What gives the rule

"Only one person can be responsible for a task! Group Responsibility - Group Irresponsibility".

◆ Regardless of the size of the task, it always has a responsible person and performers.

◆ Each area of responsibility is assigned to one person only.

◆ In the event of an error or failure of deadlines, the responsible person knows who did it, so any failure is promptly corrected.

◆ A manager who has delegated a major task only accepts the result and does not intervene in the process.

Fifteenth rule

Be proactive!

Work a hundred and two percent!

Whoever does not do more than what he's paid for will never get more than what he gets!

I earned one pound, ten shillings, and sixpence for the first review, and with that money, I bought a Persian cat. And then I got ambitious: a cat is very good, of course, but a cat is not enough. I want a car. That's it and I became a novelist.

Virginia Wolfe.

This rule applies to a topic that is important for almost any employee - promotion. We talked about transparency, remember? Well, a promotion or a salary increase is the case when a company should make...the process as clear as possible to the team.

How do employees get promoted as usual? Especially in companies without clear instructions in this regard? At best, they scramble "how to ask for a raise" and then go to the manager and experience the online recommendations.

In such articles, you can sometimes find useful tips. The person who reads them can apply them to their situation and convince the manager that they deserve the amount they are asking for. But what are the pitfalls?

People who are looking for arguments to raise their salaries online do not realize their real value to the company and their place in it. They take situations from their own experience and put them in a certain way: "It says here that management values its contribution to the company. And last month I just found us a profitable client. There is also a raise for new responsibilities. And a week ago I helped an accountant to draw up a report, although this is not my task at all".

For them, these isolated cases are just an accident. They realize that there are life cycles inside the company, and there are moments when it is necessary to move to a new level. And they try to do so.

Sometimes they succeed, and sometimes their requests are not quite justified.

Before I introduced this rule, one of the employees could come to me with such a request:

- You know, I had a son this month. The wife's on maternity leave, you know... I want a ten percent pay raise.

Everybody had their reasons: the addition to the family, the illness of a relative, even the jumping dollar rate. And it's humanly understandable that an employee needs help in such circumstances. But let's be rational: a company cannot increase its salary only due to changes in external factors. If we raise everyone's salary while maintaining the usual way of life, the business will go bankrupt.

What can we do then? Let me show you an example of how employees should formulate their requests for salary increases:

- As you know, I recently had a son. I would like to increase my salary by ten percent. Tell me, what other duties can I take on to increase my salary?

That's the key idea: an employee can't just demand money. He can't expect a raise based on his problems or work experience. On the other hand, he can take on new responsibilities and earn what he wants.

Thanks to this rule, perplexing questions like: "Why did he get a raise and not me? I have worked here as long as you have!" The team has changed its way of thinking and attitude to work.

The first step to applying for more is to work a hundred and two percent. I try to share the value of this idea with my top managers. What is it all about?

A hundred percent is the minimum that each employee has to fulfill. When an employee performs his or her duties in full, he or she works one hundred percent and receives his or her standard salary for them. To work like this is the duty of a team member to the company because these hundred percent of the work is directly proportional to his monthly salary.

Some companies have not yet been fully cleaned up. And then against the backdrop of general confusion and chaos, some employees try to stand out because they are doing all their jobs. They present their standard work as something outstanding, for which they are given a monument.

But you understand very well that this situation is not an excuse to raise salaries. On the contrary, it is a push for change at the corporate level. Under such conditions, the owner should better ask himself a question: how to make the company more efficient? And sometimes the answer will be to fire ineffective employees and revise the organizational structure.

When a company already employs a team of people whose values coincide, one can expect a sane reaction from them. It is important to convey to employees that the points in the job description are the minimum they are required to fulfill.

A hundred and two percent is the result that the employee has brought when he went beyond his position. The amount of work that he took over the norm. It could be anything:

◆ promotion of his KPI*.

◆ new responsibilities within his position.

◆ new responsibilities in related positions.

* KPI (Key Performance Indicators) is a ratio that determines the performance of an enterprise, employee, department, activity within the framework of achieving the operational or strategic goals of a company.

Me and my top managers make it clear to employees: "If you want to be singled out, do your job by a hundred and two percent. Such people will develop in the company".

Why a hundred and two? And what is one percent then? In my companies it is considered that to do a hundred and one percent job is to make it better than expected from an employee:

◆ long before the deadline.

◆ with a margin for the following tasks.

◆ with developed checklists, business processes, and other documents that the employee and colleagues will still need.

To understand what one hundred and one or two percent is, remember what criteria you use to select the best employees of the month. You have to admit that such people immediately come to mind. And you highlight them because they have done more than what is written in their job descriptions.

I'm going to deviate a little bit from the subject and tell you how we use this chip. Every month tops give the HR department the names of their wards they think are the best. Then the HR-specialists print out photos of these people and place them on a special stand for a month. These employees also receive special stickers on their laptops with the inscription "Best Employee of the Month". At the end of the year, three winners with the largest number of stickers receive holiday vouchers in another city or other prizes at a corporate New Year party.

It works smoothly. And you and I understand that the main task of this tool is to instill in employees the habit of doing more than required by the management and job description. I recommend you this rule because it works wonders. It is much nicer to work with people who ask, "What more can I do for the company?" instead of "What more can the company do for me? These are the people we want to develop; we want to thank - and money - and new perspectives.

Implement this rule in your company! Explain to the team which principle the management raises salaries. You will be surprised at what kind of productive and purposeful wards you have! Well, I am waiting for you on the next pages.

What gives the rule

"Be proactive! Work a hundred and two percent! Whoever does not do more than what he's paid for will never get more than what he gets!"

◆ Makes the pay rise transparent, eliminates rumors and discontent.

◆ Helps employees give up the harmful belief, "Everyone owes me just for working here".

◆ Shelves information to clarify the difference between a hundred and two percent.

◆ Encourages team members to develop autonomy and initiative.

Sixteenth rule

Working in a cohesive team is the key to our success.

Respect your colleagues and do not create conflicts when working as a team.

Viruses consist of pure DNA (or a similar self-replicating molecule) surrounded by a protein shell. They're all parasites. They are believed to have originated from "rebellious" genes that have been released and now travel from body to body directly through the air.

Richard Dawkins "The Selfish Gene."

The word "work" itself contains the idea that employees come to the office to devote eight hours of their time to achieving work results. That's exactly what it is and it's not. But let's be honest and see what those eight hours take. Especially in companies where corporate culture has not yet been built up.

What is it that turns out? In addition to performing production tasks and communicating with each other, employees spend a lot of time figuring out relationships, arguing, and criticizing. Most often, these are minor conflicts that fill the "grey days". You think one colleague yelled at another. Well, you bet two employees, one of them guilty, who doesn't happen? Discusses one person behind his back, and let him discuss it, it's their own business.

Well, it's not. Only at first glance do these minor conflicts not affect anything. They actually steal a significant part of the team energy. Instead of working, the employees waste their energy on skirmishes.

Let's take a broader look at the problem. It's not just that, every day employees deliberately spend two or three hours on quarrels. How will an employee feel about a company where unpleasant, conflict people are waiting for him? Will he be happy to wake up and go to work? Will he enthusiastically take on new tasks and do his job well? Will he be in the mood to work at least one hundred percent? And finally, how long will he stay in a place like this?

All this in one way or another affects the efficiency of the entire team. Whether it's one small quarrel a day or a good corporate tradition, you can agree that no employee will approach his manager with words:

- Deduct from my salary ten hours of working time I spent on quarrels and conflicts.

On the contrary, employees get their money but do not work it out until the end. That is why I am convinced that the team should be informed in advance about the atmosphere in the company. What does this atmosphere mean? Mutual respect. I will explain how this quality should it manifest itself in specific situations.

You have probably noticed that most of the training materials say that the task of a manager is to maintain a healthy microclimate in the company. They say that this trait distinguishes the leader from the boss. But is it only the task of managers?

I am a supporter of the opinion that to maintain an atmosphere of mutual respect is the daily duty not only of managers but also of ordinary employees, that is, of the whole team. The fourteenth rule is a technique that extends this idea to the whole team. Owners and managers are skeptical at first of this rule. Especially those with small teams where everything seems to be in sight. For a long time, I didn't have to implement the rule of quarreling. The team was small, and all conflicts were resolved on the spot before they could get heated.

But the company is growing. It becomes more and more difficult for management to track the relationship in each department. Yes, there is an HR-department, which takes over this function. But any HR-department functions correctly when it works, based on the foundation of a healthy corporate culture. It is true: when an HR specialist talks to an employee and tries to explain to him why it is not good to yell at a colleague, it would be good to refer to a specific rule. Otherwise, the employee may think of it as picking on his personality:

- Everybody else is yelling at each other and the remark is only for me!

This applies to any rule and we will talk about it further. In the meantime, it is important to understand one thing: to demand adequate working behavior from a team, you must define it for everyone.

That's why step number one is to announce to all wards that from now on there is no place for an emotional component in working issues. We are not moving on to personalities. When we look for the cause of a mistake, we do not blame the person, but only consider the areas of responsibility. From now on, any dialogue is conducted constructively and rationally, without shouting, clicking language, or blaming.

Let us be realistic: not all employees follow the new rule from day one. Someone in the old memory will want to solve the problem quickly - to grow in the ward and wait for a new result. From here follows step number two - talk to dissenters personally.

I call people who, contrary to the value of mutual respect, behave inappropriately as "employee-viruses". Why? Because they infect others and spread the virus of such behavior throughout the team. One can talk about such employees for a long time, it can take a separate chapter. Let me say one thing: they have many qualities that they demotivate the team with. Disrespect and the transition to identity are just a few of them.

So, it is necessary to have an "anti-virus conversation" with such people. It consists of several stages, which I will now describe.

Stage I

- In our company, it is customary to communicate with employees respectfully. When you shout at a person, he loses his motivation to work, and this reduces overall effectiveness. Do you agree? If so, will you continue to set an example with your behavior?

Stage II

- How exactly will you behave now?

If the employee's response suits you, you can proceed to the next step. If not, you should adjust the answer:

- Yes, I agree. And I would like to ask you to concentrate on the area of responsibility of the person, and not on his personality. Good?

Stage III

- Can I count on you?

Stage IV

- Let's meet in a week at the same time, and you will tell about your successes.

Stage V

The manager or HR specialist interviews at the appointed time and finds out if the employee fulfilled his promise.

If after such a conversation the employee realizes his mistake and corrects himself, we can assume that he "was cured of the virus." Not the fact that he will not get sick again. But now the leadership at least has the hope that such an employee is curable.

However, there are incurable employees. Despite all the conversations, they continue to behave as before. They nod in their eyes and agree that they need to change, but they are not making efforts. And all because being so is part of their personality.

Such traits are deeply embedded at the level of beliefs and values. But the company is not a psychotherapy center. She does not have time to change employees for herself. Therefore, my advice to you: say goodbye to employees who refuse to share common values.

When you introduce a rule, you understand in advance why. And the effectiveness of your company is much more important than the presence of "employee viruses" in it. For this reason, I have repeatedly fired not just workers, but top managers, key players! But I realized the importance of these decisions, and time showed that I was not mistaken. Time - and the general indicators of the company. If you seriously want to engage in your corporate culture and make the company a peaceful place for fruitful work, implement this rule. The overall effectiveness depends on it in many respects. Sometimes much more than it seems at first look.

What gives the rule

"Working in a close-knit team is the key to our success. Respect colleagues and do not create conflicts when working in a team"

◆ Directs team energy to work tasks and overall performance.

◆ It allows the company to rationally use its resources: if a person receives a salary, then for full work.

◆ Maintains a healthy microclimate in the company, without shifting this task exclusively to managers. Makes maintaining an atmosphere of mutual respect the goal of each team member.

◆ Teaches employees to think about their actions and reactions makes them more restrained and rational.

Seventeenth rule

A stop in self-development and learning equals gradual degradation.

Take up self-study, work on your competencies, become a professional.

Continuous learning is the key to success in the 21st century. Lifelong learning is the minimum requirement for success in your (as well as any other) field of activity.

Brian Tracy

Where self-development ends, the sofa begins.

David Allen.

The first part of the rule is a bold statement, isn't it? It sounds categorical, but I'm convinced that: if a person... doesn't develop, he degrades. Not to himself, here he remains the same as he was. But in relation to others - one hundred percent. If colleagues at work and even more so colleagues from other companies develop, a person with the position "I already know everything" falls lower and lower in the conditional "tournament table".

The market is constantly changing. It is difficult even to fix its state at a specific moment in time. Today something is considered a trend of the future, and tomorrow it is a trite banality. Every day new professional books, articles, researches are published. They are constantly rethinking views on the same things.

Remember the reception "Sell me a pen". Ten years ago, it was a breakthrough tool for America. Every second recruiter or manager asked a job seeker to sell him a pen, and he was worried about selling it.

Ask the job seeker to sell the pen today. At best, he will delicately explain to you that he has never sold a pen and this will not demonstrate his professionalism in any way. At worst, it will automatically blacklist your company. It's not a reproach to anyone, don't think about it. It's just a little indication that any instrument has an expiration date.

There must be people on your team who feel this transition from a "fresh reception" to "yesterday". This is not an outstanding skill that units have. You can develop it in anybody you want. It's all about training. How? To learn all the time.

I never stop learning myself. And I don't remember ever thinking I already know everything. It's the other way around. The more I learn, the clearer I realize that there is more to come. It all started with chaotic training sessions and books. I was so eager to learn as much as possible about the field of sales, in which I started, that attended all indiscriminately events related to this topic in my hometown.

Now I am more selective in my approach to training. But that's not the least of it in my life. It's just that if before it was a haphazard approach to any training or master class, now it's an in-depth study of each new topic.

I told all this in order to lead any business owner to the important question: if a manager is constantly learning, how can he work with people who do not?

We select a team according to our own values. If self-development is not an empty sound for us, it must also be meaningful for our team.

There is a direct link between the results of the whole company and those of each individual employee. You and I understand this, but our beneficiaries do not always. Sometimes they think that the company is a huge system that moves forward by itself, takes the employee under its wing and from that moment on accepts any results. The bad ones are no big deal, the company exists on its own and does not depend on the quality of work of one little person.

Our task is to show employees the direct connection between their efforts and the effectiveness of the company. They should understand that the speed of development of the company depends on the speed of team development. "The company moves at the speed of the weakest top manager, and the department moves at the speed of the weakest employee", remember? It would be great if your team remembers this too.

If it is important for a manager to develop his employees, his task is to weave this process into the worldview of the company. By making training a part of everyday life, you will save yourself the need to read the lectures.

With a team like children: they can talk as much as they like about the benefits of reading, but they will not like books. But if they see parents reading at home, if they see the home library, they will continue a good tradition.

So, it's necessary to take two steps here:

◆ Step one - show an example.

◆ The second step is to make learning a part of working life.

Let me give an example of my companies. First, training. I told in the ninth chapter that it is important for management to develop employees. It was about those who want to take on new responsibilities, expand or change positions. But this does not mean that employees without "vertical ambitions" can do nothing.

Everyone has to develop. In my companies, every employee attends external training events from time to time. This can be one master class, a lecture hall or even a whole course for several months. The main thing is that the knowledge is relevant for the ward and he can immediately apply it in his position.

How is this process carried out? The staff member finds the event, creates a task in the manager.

There he adds his manager, explains to him the need for this program at the moment or in the future. The manager gets acquainted with the event and makes a verdict whether or not the employee should go there.

Usually managers choose to "go" because the employees have learned to find really important and quality events. Next, the company fully or partially pays for the visit, and the employee with a calm soul goes to get new knowledge.

When they return, they are obliged to write a detailed report on their training. The report is the answer to three questions:

◆ What have I learned?

◆ What have I learned?

◆ What will I apply?

This is not to make sure that an employee has not missed an event, but to ensure that the rest of the employees benefit from the benefits that their colleague has received. Such reports are seen by everyone. The specialists from different departments, therefore, have a rough idea of what is going on in the related areas.

Another good thing is corporate training. This is needed when the whole team needs the same skill. For the whole team it can be planning or time management. For the top management of their departments, interaction between themselves and oratory skills. Variants of the sea. All training records - online and offline - we upload to the corporate

YouTube channel whenever possible. Every employee has access to it.

Now my team at the 4Smart Business Academy conducts corporate training itself.

How else can I develop my employees? To equip them with the right books and make reading part of the work process! Our office shelf with literature has grown into a full-fledged corporate library over time. There are paper, electronic and audio versions of books there. There are editions for any specialty and any skill. And the most important thing is that the library is constantly replenished.

With reading the same system works as with training activities, but even better. Do you know why? Because for every book you read an employee receives an award! To do this you have to write a report according to the same scheme as after the training.

That's it. Every month an employee gets as much as he earned by his perseverance for performing such a simple ritual. But for better information assimilation, we recommend reading no more than two books per month. One book in two weeks is a solid figure.

At the end of the year, at the New Year's Eve, the company once again encourages its "bookwormers". The gifts go to the most reading department and five employees with the most books read.

Training at the expense of the company and encouragement for reading is one of our many chips. They serve as an excellent PR among friends and acquaintances. But more importantly, they develop the team and make it more professional. And all through the game and the competition element.

Do you want to create a huge library? Pay the team a subscription to a book app. The main thing is not just to require employees to learn, but also to provide them with resources and conditions.

Now that you know a couple of tricks to motivate you to learn, it will be easier to implement this in your own. Of course, if you consider it important and see a direct link to the results of the whole company. I suggest you do it for the sake of the experiment. I can assure you that no one has ever worked worse from new knowledge. So good luck with your implementation!

What gives the rule

"A stop in self-development and learning equals gradual degradation. Learn yourself, work on your competencies, become a professional."

◆ Shows the link between employee self-development and overall company performance. Focuses the team's attention on training.

◆ Keeps people from sitting quietly at their desks, solving tasks through the same activities year after year.

◆ Trains employees to be flexible, allowing them to adapt more quickly to change.

◆ Gives professionals a wide range of tools.

Eighteenth rule

Find out your EPR (employee's performance result) and work on its achievement!

Now EPR is an incomprehensible acronym for you. But I am sure that by the end of this chapter you will seriously consider implementing this rule in the company. Of course, if it is important for you to understand what you pay your employees for.

What is EPR? It is the result of an employee's activity. It's what the company expects of him. It is the result of the work that assumes a specific position in a particular company.

Why is it important to outline the result of each employee's work and to focus on it all the time? Because otherwise, you will get many processes that may not lead to the desired result.

During our training programs, my colleagues and I constantly ask the audience what is the result of the activity of this or that specialist. Is this the EPR of a salesman? There are a variety of options from the hall:

◆ to go to meetings;

◆ to sell the product;

◆ to make the customer satisfied;

◆ to call the base.

Do you think these are the right answers? No, they're not. The result of the seller's activity is the profit from his transactions. Note: "profit from transactions" - is the end result, and "go, sell, do, call" - processes. An employee can go to meetings all month, wildly tired, stay in the office late. But if all his efforts did not lead to sales, then there is no result.

Each owner must determine what EPR he expects from each position in his business. Because much depends on the specifics of the company and its objectives. In our company I expect profit from sellers, and other managers expect the maximum number of contracts from the same position.

Again, it may seem like something painfully simple. Obviously, a salesman is hired to bring in money. Believe me: it's not so obvious to the employees. At work, they live inside dozens of tasks. They have to do many things at the same time.

For them, it's a victory to just take the time to work on several tasks at once. For them, the achievement is to stay longer and work longer. When a company introduces the result of an employee's activity and starts asking employees about the results of the tasks, they may be outraged:

- What does "no result" mean? I stayed at work, I did most of the work here, I helped my colleagues! And you are telling me that I did not do any good?!

The result of the activity is the first thing I demand to check-in interviews. Earlier than experience, skills, personal qualities and anything else. Our recruiters start the conversation with that question:

- In our company, we have such a concept as EPR - the result of the employee's activity. EPR seamstresses - a sewn dress. EPR baker - baked bread. EPR janitors - clean room. And what is EPR in your position? And what was in your previous job?

This is where the candidate's ability to produce results is shown. Even more, the way a person thinks: does he understand why he is working, is able to formulate goals and achieve them. What is the job for him: to achieve specific results or simply to imitate a rapid activity?

I will discuss the main criteria of the EPR.

◆ Formulation as a result, not a process.

Not "call", but "number of calls", not "wash the floor", but "clean the floor".

◆ It can be measured.

It is always a clear number of something.

◆ An employee can be influenced by him.

It is not fair to demand the same cleaner from the same salesman. It is brought by several departments at once, not by him alone. It is therefore necessary to formulate the EPR of the beneficiary in such a way that he is able to achieve this result.

◆ The employee knows his EPR and agrees with him.

This is also important, because if you expect money from the seller and he categorically does not consider it to be his result, the company will not be able to work efficiently. The employee will be able to bring a quality result when he understands its value and is confident in its attainability.

Not all owners are immediately permeated by the idea of EPR. They have the conviction:

-An employee works - don't touch him.

Only if the owner has taken seriously the efficiency of the company and wants to be sure that he hired a good team, he still needs to go deeper into the topic. Yes, the employee is working. But works how? Good, not good, intermittent, obviously bad? What are the criteria for assessing his work?

It all becomes easier when every employee has a performance result in the company. In this case, the management no longer thinks about how exactly the ward works. If you have achieved a result - you work well, if you have not achieved it - badly.

It is important that all RDSs are prescribed and communicated to every person in the company. Employees should know what is required of them. And most importantly, it will allow them to focus on the end result at once. They will understand that all their processes must lead to the result. Then people will not be obsessed only with execution. They will perceive the work processes not as self-sufficient goals, but as intermediate stages. The final stage is always the result.

There's more. Every employee should have the result of the activity: from the owner to the office manager. Let me give an example of how we defined the performance results for certain positions.

◆ EPR Recruiter - employees hired according to requirements, who have passed the probation period with a personal result.

Note: do not "conduct interviews", do not "process resumes". Only staff members who have completed their probationary period. You can simply hire as many employees as you wish. But the value of a recruiter is that the team is complemented by a cool specialist, and preferably for a long time.

◆ EPR of the personal assistant to the manager is the maximum free time of the manager.

Not to keep a manager's schedule, not to organize meetings, not to accompany him during negotiations. All these processes should free up time. If the supervisor feels that he or she has some free time, then the assistant is doing his or her job.

◆ EPR HR specialist is a loyal and motivated team of professionals who work for results.

Not to organize corporate parties, not to buy gifts and not to solve conflicts. These and other actions should have an ultimate goal.

◆ EPR Executive Director - goals and plans of the company, achieved and implemented by a team of professionals through the implementation of effective management tools within the framework of regular management.

It sounds difficult because the executive director has a high position and many responsibilities. Therefore, it is especially important for him to know his EPR, so that he does not spread his attention to many areas of responsibility.

For me, the value of the DDS is obvious. I hope you are also sympathetic to this idea. A logical question: where should the owner of the company start? As usual, with yourself. I recommend starting from top to bottom. When you have prescribed all the EPR, I advise you to transfer them to the organizational structure of the company. Let all employees see their performance and the EPR of their colleagues. This eliminates the questions "Who is to set the task?" or "Why am I the only one asked for the result?". I propose to conduct a small experiment, which shows whether you need to introduce the EPR in your company or not. Write down the results of two or three employees with whom you work closely. Write down what exactly you pay them money for. Then walk up to them, tell them about the DDS on the example of a seamstress or a baker and ask about the performance of their positions.

How similar were your definitions? Do employees understand correctly what the company pays them for? If the results are different, this is a good reason to implement such a tool.

Think about whether everyone in your team is making a difference. Does everyone bring it as much as they could? If there are reliable specialists on your team, they can use their potential to the maximum. But to do so, they need to set an example. EPR is the example that will make your company more efficient. Implement it, and see for yourself!

What gives the rule

"Find out your EPR (employee performance) and work on achieving it!"

◆ Employees focus on results, not processes.

◆ Only the most productive people remain in the company. Those who imitated the job quickly expose themselves and eventually leave on their own.

◆ There is certainty in the team. Everyone understands what he or she should do and what his or her colleagues should do.

◆ The management assesses everyone according to a predetermined criterion - the result of the activity.

Nineteenth rule

Discipline is the key to the success of the company and a sign of professionalism. Be a role model!

Motivation lights you up, but it doesn't do a single thing. Discipline, intent, strong habit, that's what makes a case.

So, you don't have to read books about character and courage. Don't ask any more questions. Don't think about it, don't read about it. Don't talk about it with your friends. Just go and do it! Eat right and work like Carlo's dad. That's it!

Elliot Hulls.

We're already in the middle of a book. In that time, you've learned almost two dozen new corporate rules. Some of them seriously interested you, and you even plan to implement them. And indeed: they promise that the company will become more efficient and employees more responsible. I subscribe to every word written here. But you know what? It's not gonna work, unless discipline comes along with the rules.

The most terrible thing for a rule is its formal implementation (you have already seen this phrase here). Simply because "it's the right thing to do." This is from the opera "Five Signs of a Successful Company". Some people think that in business there are mandatory things, once implemented, the company will immediately become rich and famous. But the longer a man is in business, the more skeptical he is of such things... "recipes for success."

The tools or rules themselves are worth nothing. They're just words. Their real value can be seen only by starting to follow them, by applying them in practice. To do this, a company must be disciplined. That's why I put it in a separate rule.

The result depends directly on the discipline. Why? Let's have a look at it. Let's say that you have introduced a rule in the company that from now on all employees must report on the execution of tasks in the "Best case" format. You do not just implement the rule - you have a specific goal. You want to make the team responsible for its decisions and define the boundaries between the tasks of the delegator and the executor. This is an inconvenient rule. It ruins the comfort zone of many employees who are used to shifting responsibility. Of course, they will try to avoid following this rule. At first, they will do it the same way. And the biggest mistake of the management will be to indulge it:

"Well, this is a really complicated rule. Everything has to be done gradually..."

With this position of the owner and top management, employees will understand two things:

1. The rule is just a formality. In fact, it can be omitted.

2. The manager or the owner is not responsible for his or her words, so his or her requests may not be taken seriously in the future.

More often than not, employees draw such conclusions subconsciously. But somehow it undermines the authority of managers. Will they speak out in front of everyone or keep everything to themselves - the main thing that they will doubt. To prevent this from happening, along with innovations, one should take care of discipline.

It is up to each company to choose how it controls order. Some penalize non-compliance with the rules, others encourage compliance, while others issue warnings. But no matter what policy the company chooses, there are universal steps that will not stop it.

Step one is to obey the rules yourself.

If the company has a rule to solve non-working issues outside of working hours, and you constantly distract employees by talking about fishing on weekends, they will do the same.

To you it is possible, means, not so all strictly. If you do not want this attitude to the rules, first of all, observe them yourself.

Step two is to convince top managers to follow the rules the business owner can't control every member of the team. But he can make the top allies who will be...

broadcast the importance of the rules to their teams.

It's important. The team shouldn't take innovation as an owner's whim: "Oh, he's got something for himself again..." Such statements and moods need to be processed immediately.

But you will not personally go from department to department and listen to who reacted to the new rule. Your top managers must process employee objections. Processing does not mean saying: "You still have no choice". Processing objections is to convey once again the importance of the rule for the company and for the "rebellious" employee in particular.

The rules will never take root if they are not believed by the tops themselves. Therefore, even at the design stage, top managers must be involved in the process. If they do not penetrate this idea, they will agree with you through "do not want", and then close with the team in the office and say:

- Guys, we are again being asked to report in the best possible way. I know its bullshit; it pisses me off. But let's play along because I can't fight it.

It's a typical "employee-virus" quote. And now you lower the toxicity of this type of employee, especially in management positions. So, surround yourselves with like-minded people.

Step three, control the rules.

To do this, you need to assign a responsible employee who will monitor the implementation of the rule. And another important point in the discipline is to react immediately to violations. In our companies, this happens according to the following principle: if a person violates the rule in public, he can be reprimanded in public. But in most cases, the manager does not have to take it out in public.

The point is to make employees understand that the company does not do anything for show. This is by no means a dictatorship. Believe me, people who share your values will support your rules. Not because you are more important and you have to obey, but because they see their value to the company. If the employees take their work seriously and want to develop internally, they will support any improvement.

Think about the rules that already exist in your company. Vowels or not - they are. If you are confident in their usefulness for the business and the team, follow the discipline of their implementation. And introduce new rules to get better. On the following pages, I will give you a dozen or two more ideas.

Only the discipline of execution leads to the result. And to get closer to your goal step by step, you need to control the implementation. Remember this when you decide to introduce an important rule for the company.

What gives the rule

"Discipline is the key to the success of the company and a sign of professionalism. Be a role model!"

◆ Shows employees that the company has serious intentions, and innovation is not a formality.

◆ Provides the result for which the rule was initially introduced.

◆ Helps to implement the rules.

◆ Increases the probability of achieving the objectives.

Twentieth rule

Thank you and praise your colleagues, dealers and customers around you more often.

When I see that people do not smile at me, I just start to smile and say hello to them, and as if by magic, more smiling people appear around me.

It turns out that the world, like a mirror, reflects you.

Robert Kiyosaki.

"Rich Dad, Poor Dad."

The words of encouragement and hello may be short, but they have an endless echo.

Mother Teresa.

I know what you're thinking: "It's okay to report on tasks, plan time and create a corporate library.

But what does that have to do with praise?"

Well, don't be surprised. Acknowledgment and praise have the same effect on the overall effectiveness of a company as all of the above. People like to be praised. What benefits does it bring to business owners and executives? People want to be good in the eyes of others. And when those around them openly notice it, people want to support this opinion about themselves.

How do words of praise work? They focus the employee's attention on the line of praise for which he has been praised. When he hears these words of praise, he tries to do the same thing again so he can be praised again.

Do you want the employee to come to work on time? Praise him for the time he got here first. Do you want the employee to remember to write daily reports? Tell him.

"Thank you" when he sends a report on the task at the appointed time. Do you want the newcomer to read more and improve in his specialty? Evaluate his book report and say that he has a clear talent for distinguishing the main thing.

The important point is: if you can, do it in public. I am sure that you and your top managers are equally interested in all team members achieving good performance on all parameters. If it is important for the company that your employees are not late, you need to make it clear to the whole team. If the company has decided that everyone should read and learn, there is more than one employee.

Therefore, praise and thank you for your discipline and achievements with everyone! This will give a double result. First, when people see how they praise their colleague, they will think: "I can do it too! Now I will come to work earlier too, and I too will be praised. Or at least I'll be as good as my colleague."

Secondly, it will create a new system of relationships in the company. Gradually, the employees will rearrange their manner of communication. Subconsciously they will find something good in the interlocutors, for which you can give them a compliment or say "thank you". Let them be the little things, but they are what our daily life consists of. Thank you for the printed document, for the door held, for the tea brewed - all of this makes the staff feel better.

When employees experience positive emotions at work, they associate being in the office with something joyful. In the long term, this loyalty to the company will benefit you. The team will feel more comfortable with the changes. People will no longer view any innovation as an attempt to harm them. They will understand the topic before they resist. This is really important. A company that wants to develop will change itself one way or another. It can be anything: the management system, the time of arrival at work, the office itself... Any news is better communicated to the "heated" team that is ready to accept them. Consider the tradition of praise and thanksgiving to employees as a way of making them "warm" customers, as in sales. A good salesperson does not just sell a product - he builds a relationship.

What else does this rule do? It pulls employees out of their routine and allows them to look around. I often hear complaints from business owners that their colleagues do not see their role in the overall process. So why not fix it? It is possible to praise colleagues in public for their work achievements.

How do we do it? Monthly meetings! This is where every top manager regularly thank their wards for their contribution. In addition to the top thanks are expressed by the CEO and the owner. As a result, for one hour of meetings, many employees receive their portion of deserved praise. Employees are proud of the fact that they were noted - this time. And they do not want to lower the bar next month - this is two.

Praise and thank you for your work at meetings are the best way to show the team where the company is going and what other colleagues are doing. The employee is focused on his tasks. He knows about someone else's work only from common projects or personal communication with a couple of friends. Mark everyone's achievements in the context of the whole company, and from now on everyone will start taking their functions more seriously.

So, monthly meetings. But why wait a whole month if public praise and efficiency can be increased much more often? Start a general corporate chat in any messenger. I'm pretty sure you already have one. Only now write there about all the victories - serious and small - there. Assign this credit to the whole team and individual employees who performed the tasks.

I regularly throw in our chat screenshots of messages from customers who write me words of gratitude for our programs or performances. This is a common victory, and I share it with everyone. That's what my colleagues do. Often employees themselves share their achievements in the general chat. They know that they are genuinely happy for them, and not perceived as an upstart.

By the way, the achievements don't have to just be workers. You and your team can share everything with each other: good grades in external training, a completed project for a client or a new record in a morning jog. Why not rejoice at the achievements of your colleagues?

You understand: when everyone in the company thinks positively, but they transpose this mood to customers and dealers. That's why the rule also applies to this part of the job. If you do not want to provide services, but really help, teach your team to notice the positive in your customers and dealers.

If your calls or letters are associated with a "nice guy" from the last conversation, they will be more willing to communicate and open the letters. These are not manipulative tricks. They are human relationships in which everyone wants to be.

Implement this rule, and cultivate positive thinking in your employees. Let them follow you and learn to notice and highlight the good in others. Then they will more often give reason to praise and thank you.

What gives the rule

"Thank and praise your colleagues, dealers and customers around you more often."

◆ Focuses employees' attention on what the company needs.

◆ Makes employees' thinking positive: they focus on the good and notice it from each other in the first place.

◆ Pulls specialists out of a "vacuum": shows how important their role is in the overall process.

◆ Makes a team loyal to the leadership and its decisions.

◆ Shapes the human relationship between the company and the client. Excludes the option where the client will not want to contact you next time because of poor service.

Twenty-first rule

You give the assignment, make sure it's understood correctly by asking a colleague about it.

If you accept the task, ask enough questions to complete it.

Judge a man more by his questions than by his answers.

François Voltaire.

The main thing is not to stop asking questions.

Albert Einstein.

We have approached two basic processes in the work of any company - statement and acceptance of tasks. Nobody is afraid of them until there is a force majeure, which suffers the result. It can be anything: ordered the wrong batch of goods, hired the wrong contractor, bought the wrong tickets.

How often do they do this? They look for the guilty. The supervisor or person responsible for the task restores everything: who turned to whom, what said, how he was answered, etc. We have already discussed this, remember? Only then did all the troubles come from the fact that there were many responsible people in the task and everyone shifted the blame on each other.

Now the situation is different. There is a responsible person, a performer too, but something is wrong. This is something - a misunderstanding between the parties. I wouldn't surprise you if I said that all people are different. It's usually a phrase that gets past your ears, which is a painfully obvious thought. But I do recommend that you think about these words and apply them to work situations.

In my companies, top managers and I also wondered: why does this happen? In what business process is there an error? Where did we miss something? And the answer was found at the very beginning. That's why we revised the way we should set and accept tasks.

It is good that in companies this happens regularly, because any scheme can be tested and improved.

Now we have final versions, the effectiveness of which has been confirmed at least in my companies. So, they are implemented at the corporate level. It is a kind of GOST: the way to act ideally. An employee on his own initiative can deviate from the given order, but the responsibility for the unexpected result will lie on him.

What kind of rules are these? The first one concerns delegation. When an employee sets a task for an employee, he or she must ask a question:

- Tell me, how did you understand the task?

It is this suggestion that can correct errors and remove misunderstandings at an early stage. We are different, and sometimes we understand different things too. Especially if it is a new task for the employee or if he is a newcomer.

Notice: the question sounds exactly in the open. There's no point in asking, "Do you understand the task?". Even if the employee answers in the affirmative, it is not the fact that he is telling the truth. He may do it so as not to appear foolish or to hit his face in the dirt during his probationary period. So, give the person the opportunity to say what he's learned to himself.

There are wards who are the first to speak:

- So, I take it I have to do this and that to get this?

It's a good habit. It is desirable that every employee who has even a little doubt about the task should ask this question. But you know for a fact that not everyone does that. So, if your companies need to tighten up the deregulation process, teach your employees to ask the executors how they understood the task.

However, you also remember that the responsibility for accepting the task lies with the contractor. It is up to him to find out all the details, if the delegate has not specified them first. So that this does not turn into an improvisation every time, I give you a list of mandatory questions for task acceptance. Thanks to these questions, the performer will know all the details in order to have a complete idea of what he or she is going to do.

Deadline.

A task without a deadline is not a task. That's why you need to know the deadline first.

Priority.

For the person who sets the task, it is the most necessary and important, and to make it preferably "for yesterday". But the performer has a dozen others in addition to the new task. In order to plan the load correctly, he should immediately find out the priority of the task.

You should ask your immediate superior about the priority of the task over other tasks. It is he who must decide in which sequence the tasks should be performed.

Final goal

I've already said enough about the goal in a separate chapter. It is important for the performer to understand his role in the chain of actions. If the task is a routine one, this question may not be necessary. But most of the time, it is still needed. A person will know how to do the task better if he or she understands the final goal.

Intermediate control points.

Control Points are a tool for long-term multistage tasks. It is also needed for beginners who do not yet have enough experience. How does it work? The performer agrees that on certain days, he will provide the manager with intermediate results - something he has already done.

This will allow the delegator to correct the ward's actions in time and avoid errors. If the assignment is new and complex, control points are needed.

The important point is that at the appointed time the performer must provide the result himself. The Delegate should not be the first to ask him where the job is, if the deadline has not yet arrived. Only after the deadline can he find out where the promised result is.

Why is that? Because it cultivates responsibility in the performer and does not demotivate him with constant invasion by the manager.

The ability to delegate all or part of a task.

If the task is large and there are many different actions, it is quite possible that for greater efficiency some part of it should be delegated to a specialist. He or she may work in the company, or may be an external contractor. The main thing is to learn about the necessity of such actions in advance.

Possible budget, responsible for payment, payment method

If money plays a key role in the task, it is better to find out in advance who will allocate it and when. This will save time in the future so that you do not have to run from employee to employee and find out who is responsible for the finances. There can be many sources: the company's cash register, the manager's personal account, a job card. It is necessary to find out at the stage of accepting the task.

The contractor should talk about how he understood the task.

As I said, any performer is better off making it his good habit.

"Anything else?"

This magic question the performer should ask at the very end. Thanks to it, the delegator usually remembers important details that he forgot to say immediately.

We got eight questions. It is not so much, and in real communication on their clarification takes no more than three to five minutes.

If you compare this to the hypothetical time it will take to redo the wrong result, it is better to invest in taking the task responsibly.

If you find this rule useful for your company, implement it. I assure you; you will not need many resources. Except for patience, but it is an obligatory part of any change. I wish you and your employees to distribute their time efficiently. Remember: setting and accepting tasks are not processes that are worth saving on.

What gives the rule

"If you give the assignment, make sure it's understood correctly by asking a colleague about it. "If you accept an assignment, ask enough questions to do it."

◆ Allows for more "on shore" to agree on all the nuances that could lead to a mistake.

◆ Allows the performer from the first time to make a complete picture of what is happening and to understand his role in the task.

◆ Insures both sides from mistakes related to misunderstanding or silence of information about the task.

◆ Teaches the team to interact competently with each other and focus on the result.

Twenty-second rule

A delighted client is the highest priority in any of the actions of each employee.

Work so that we are recommended.

It's not the employer who gives the salary, the employer only distributes the money. Salary is given by the client.

Henry Ford.

The key to success is to create realistic expectations for customers, which then must not just be met, but surpassed.

Richard Branson.

Whatever services you provide, you'll get a wow-effect. Something must impress the customer so that he understands how much attention to detail you pay.

Carl Sewell, Paul Brown.

"Clients for life."

Tell me, how many client orientations books have you seen? More than one, I think. This is a really popular topic in current management, which I am sincerely glad. Business understands that simply to give to the client the declared service is not enough. He needs to be delighted to do something that will make him recommend this company to everyone I know and come back next time.

Why are companies trying so hard to be client-oriented? Because the client pays their employees' salaries. It's not the management, it's the client. The company only accumulates the funds it receives. Given the competition and struggle for the client in each niche, the company should stand out, including through its interaction with the customer.

When a business wants to be the best for the client, what does it do first? It concentrates on its sales department - on customer relations specialists. It all makes sense: these employees communicate with customers eight hours a day.

But tell me, does the sales department alone affect the degree of customer admiration? As it turns out, no. In addition to salespeople, there are many other positions in the company that somehow come into contact with the customer. These are accounting, service, logistics, warehouse, etc. It turns out that almost all departments of the company interact with the client.

On this topic, there is a great viral story about a pimple girl. It was spread on the Internet by a guy who came to the store popular clothing network and asked the girl consultant if you can pick him a coat of another size. She looked at him indifferently and said:

- No, you can't!

This is how the efforts of the longest chain of employees of a large corporation were chopped off in the last phase. And because of who? Because of the consultant - the final "seller" of the goods. Just think about how many resources the company has invested to make and put in the shop this coat: create a model, sew, bring to the open shop, run an advertising campaign... But the fate of the goods decided pimply girl consultant.

Yes, the example is rough, so it went viral. But the speed of its distribution on the network indicates that the topic is sick... The business owners understood the key idea:

- No matter how cool the product is and no matter how much effort and money the company has invested in it, its fate depends on the staff who will interact with the client.

In the girl's place could have been a rude security guard or a rude courier. But one way or another, it is these people who influence the impression of the whole company. It seems that almost nothing depends on them, but they are not.

I am a former salesman myself and I know very well how important the sales or customer service department is to most companies. It is he who makes the most of the profits for the business. I recommend to all entrepreneurs to start systematization from this department. If you improve the processes only there, the work already becomes more effective. But at the same time, I see a huge responsibility for the customer experience on every employee, from the top manager to the cleaners. That's why I made this rule in the company.

Of course, our salespeople are the first to make customers their top priority. I say more: they like it.

They get high from the reaction they get from their intention to make customers happy.

I don't make that up. We have a "Dream Team World of Libra" page on Facebook, and our HR specialists have launched a section with stories of employees who have been working in the company for many years. What have I noticed in the stories of my colleagues? Almost all of them, without conspiracy, say the same phrase:

- My main goal in the company is to make my clients happy.

To do this, they often answer the phone when the working day is long over. They choose their own gifts for their holidays and personally check that everything has been delivered on time. All to make sure that the customer enjoys working with us.

Our salesmen know that their result is money in the company's account. But they themselves admit that this is not their ultimate goal. More importantly, a satisfied client who tells his friends:

- Look, appealed to the "World of Libra", to their employee. Professionally does his job and at the same time treats in a human way, rather than tantalizing the learned script. I will buy more!

Other employees who are not directly involved in sales also read these stories. In addition, they see this rule on the walls of the office and hear from top managers about its importance. And that's why any ordinary employee invests in a customer relationship in the same way. Though less often, but if the occasion appears, he has no right to be indifferent.

How can ordinary employees show attention to customers? In business correspondence, in response to comments on social networks. If a customer comes to visit our office, the first employee can offer tea or coffee. If the customer gets lost on the way to the office, any employee can go outside and meet them. All these little things eventually form a common view of the company.

Your salesperson can spend half an hour with the customer and pick up the right product, help pay for it and send the product ahead of schedule. But if the courier at the customer's door is asking for a tip, the customer will remember that moment. And all previous efforts will be erased from his memory.

What's the conclusion? Tell each employee that it is the customers who pay him his salary. And that each team member affects the client's final impression of the entire company. When the employees are aware of their role in the process, they will stop being routine or being polite formally, "because it is necessary".

Yes, every specialist has their own EPR. But don't let him forget that regardless of the position, everyone has another serious result - a delighted client. I wish you good luck in implementing this rule!

What gives the rule

"A delighted client is the highest priority in every employee's action. Work so that we are recommended."

◆ Brings to the staff the truth about who really pays their salaries.

◆ Shows that they're not out of the process. Even if they are not sellers, they still need to be able to work with clients.

◆ Makes you take responsibility for your work and see your contribution to the company's total profit.

Twenty-third rule

Every employee is the face of the company.

A reputation that has been gained over the years can be ruined in one evening.

Don't let yourself get away with it!

Be careful with the strong drinks. They can make you shoot the tax collector... and miss.

Robert Heinline.

Good fame runs, and the skinny one flies.

One of my employees broadcast on all possible channels that everyone in the team is equally important. He was speaking at conferences with presentations on team building and respect for employees. He gave thanksgiving speeches to his team at monthly meetings. And then it turned out that he could say to his mentees: "Go out and knock before you come in" or "I'm not your boss, go to someone else with your problems".

This sketch well illustrates rule number twenty-three: "Every employee is the face of the company. A reputation that has been built up over the years can be ruined in one evening. Don't let yourself get hurt!" So, make sure yours doesn't run counter to what you say.

It's also a rule about the place of alcohol on vacation with colleagues. Usually, companies don't discuss the subject, let alone introduce it at the corporate level.

All people know that in the presence of colleagues and management do not need to get drunk and let yourself be overwhelmed. But does everyone really do this?

It so happens that behavior at the corporate level is an ethical issue. And ethical guidelines are perceived by people as recommendations, not laws. So, the employee is guided by the situation: he watches others and decides how much to drink and how to behave.

Of course, corporate behavior is primarily determined by the company's values and specifics. In a company with stricter and more conservative traditions, joint rest is reserved. In companies that promote equality and freedom of expression, people allow themselves to relax and "break away".

I certainly do not consider my companies to be the first type. On the contrary, I want all my employees to consider their team as seven. But that doesn't mean I encourage drunken antics, nicknames and vulgarity. Therefore, along with all democratic values that are directed at people and their development, I have introduced this rule in the company.

The Managing Owner of a business or SEO is the person who leads by example. It is from high positions that change begins. Imagine: a manager who has been teaching his employees to communicate respectfully for a whole year, who has eradicated the transition to personalities, suddenly gets drunk at a corporate New Year's Eve. In this state, his behavior and values change dramatically. It doesn't look consistent, does it?

I will tell you the story of another New Year's Eve corporation, where employees from all branches of the country have gathered. There was almost everyone in the hall, from the management to the warehouse workers. In the middle of the evening, one of the deputy directors was so dispersed that he went to fraternize with the warehouse guys:

- Come on, dude, pour it!

They were drinking on the bruderscape and hugging all night. At the corporate party it looked quite organic - everybody was having fun, and nobody gave special importance to the new friendship.

But what happened the next working day, when everyone sobered up and returned to work? A guy from a warehouse came up to the top company, slammed on the shoulder of yesterday's interlocutor and said: "Brother, when are we going for a beer?"

Basically, it's not a desperate situation. The supervisor can explain in private to the person that the subordination should be respected at work and act with restraint. However, it is better to make sure that such conversations are not necessarily beforehand.

So, if you are aware of your particular reaction to alcohol, I suggest two options. The first is to limit the amount. Define for yourself the boundary between just fun and unnecessary actions and try not to go for it. The second option - limit your stay in the corporate. Stay there for a while, and then wish everyone a great holiday and go to a more private place.

In many companies, corporates are perceived as team building. Management believes that the next meal will kill two birds: give the team relaxation and at the same time strengthen its corporate spirit. This is partly true. People will really relax if a couple of times a year to relax in an informal atmosphere, talk, drink at a large feast, where they celebrate a common significant event. But will it strengthen the team?

It is worth separating corporate and team building. The company needs both of these events because they both have specific goals. Teambuilding is about team building through teamwork. Drinking and eating is not the goal that unites a team for new achievements. Teambuilding is much more effective when it is teamwork with a clear and understandable end result.

HR-specialists advise organizing teambuilding in such a way that employees achieve some result together. Not just eat hamburgers, ride horses or play soccer, but do something useful together. The team can plant a tree, paint a fence or go to a master class on cooking maki. The essence of it is to learn something together, share responsibilities and gain useful experience.

However, this rule is not only about rest. It is also about the image of the company that your employees form outside of it. In external training programs, negotiations, various events, one employee becomes the representative of the whole company, its face. All the more so if he displays it with a corporate badge or badge.

It is necessary to inform your employees that when they go alone to an external event, they are a delegation from the whole company. So, they definitely shouldn't pry people on break to get to the coffee machine. You don't have to be late and let the strange lines go. And even more so, there is no need to discuss your colleagues, management and commercial details.

You can broadcast the value of mutual respect in your company for years. But people around you will never know about it if the only channel of communication with your business is an employee who interrupts the speaker. You can cultivate self-development in the company, but others will make their own conclusions if your colleague claims left and right:

- I was dragged to this event by force, I did not want to come here.

If you are already working with like-minded people who share the company's values and mission, convey to them the importance of reputation. As long as they are in your company, they cannot completely separate personal from worker when they are surrounded by unfamiliar people. Each of them is the face of the company.

No owner or manager builds a corporate culture for no reason. He wants like-minded people in his company who share the manager's approach to work and consider it ideal for them. If you agree with this opinion, take a look at this rule. Perhaps it is the rule that is missing in your corporate foundation to achieve harmony.

What gives the rule

"Every employee is the face of the company. A reputation that has been gained over the years can be ruined in one evening.

Don't let yourself get hurt!"

◆ Brings clarity to the issue of shared vacation behavior. Translates the topic from an ethical plane that allows doubt into an imperative plane.

◆ Builds the right attitude to rest in the company: it should be such that after it is not ashamed to come to the office. In this way, the team does not waste energy on unnecessary worries, but puts them into work.

Twenty-fourth rule

Take responsibility. Learn to be a leader.

Only a leader can be responsible for his words, actions, successes and failures!

I invented my own staff selection method: I was looking for people who were captains of student teams back in college. These people are natural leaders.

Jack Stack.

On a large American job search portal there is my article "Who is the leader and why it is important to be". In it, I list the main qualities of a leader and explain how this type of leader is different from the boss - the complete opposite. Read the whole article when you have a moment. I will now recap her main idea with a few sentences. The point is that the leader always takes responsibility and teaches his team.

In the previous rules, we talked a lot about responsibility for the task. But is that all we have to do? To take responsibility is not only to confirm that your name will be in the "Performer" column. To take responsibility means to be responsible for any result, including failure.

There was a discussion in the comments to the article. The readers were divided into two camps. Some believe that a leader must be born. Others believe that leadership skills can be nurtured. I am a supporter of the second option.   In my opinion, the theory of innate leadership is an excuse not to take responsibility:

- Well, I'm sorry I screwed up the task. It's how I was born...

I also often hear the view that leadership is a purely American idea. And in our spaces, people will always justify themselves and protect themselves. It's a mentality, you can't write anything.

This is why I constantly explain to my employees: everyone can be a leader. Regardless of the position held, a person has to be responsible for his or her actions. This is healthy behavior of an adult.

Of course, my companies occasionally have employees who do not reach this rank. They are in almost every business. If they fail, they find twenty reasons why someone is to blame and not them. The customer did not pay on time, the courier did not deliver, a colleague is overdue - everyone is to blame.

What does a leader do if he fails? He asks himself:

"What have I done wrong? What do I have to do next time to be different? How can I fix the situation now?" Everyone has the right to make a mistake, we are all human beings. For some people only, mistakes are valuable lessons, and for others they're a reason to complain about a hard life or blame someone.

Among employers, there is a perception that between a job seeker with career failures and an applicant with an ideal reputation to choose in favor of the former. Professionals with "fack-up" are more experienced than employees with "excellent" syndrome.

I do not take this idea as an axiom. But I admit that sometimes this opinion justifies itself - in cases when employees with failures had enough responsibility and self-criticism to learn from their failures. People who blame external factors for their failures will never make business more efficient and profitable. They will only slow down its development.

Employees are often clichéd. They believe that only in high positions you need to worry about your inner qualities and train yourself to be responsible.

And ordinary employees simply do their job - no more and no less. This is a destructive approach.

The place in the hierarchy is not an indicator. I am sure that the leader must be every employee who has at least one task. If he is commissioned to do it, then he takes it on completely, with the possibility of error.

Yes, top managers and executives must be leaders - yet the efficiency of the whole departments depends on them, and here one cannot afford to experiment. But other colleagues should not fall behind as well. The responsibility of the wards for their successes and failures is as important for the company as their professionalism and loyalty.

It is to some extent interesting to take care of the employees' mistakes: experience, new cases... But for the business to develop and work effectively, it is better to teach people in your team to behave in an adult way. And this rule is perfectly suited for this purpose!

What gives the rule

"Take responsibility. Learn to be a leader. Only a leader can be responsible for his words, actions, good luck and failures!"

◆ Expands the concept of responsibility for employees: not only for the task, but also for its outcome.

◆ Shows employees what management thinks about their excuses and accusations about external factors.

◆ Frees management from having to explain why the employee has not been promoted despite all his loyalty or professionalism.

◆ Makes accountability an integral part of any employee, not just top management representatives.

Twenty-fifth rule

Keep statistics of tasks completed and evaluate your personal effectiveness!

The problem is that we focus on those rare cases when our methodology works and almost never on the numerous examples of its failure.

Nassim Nicholas Taleb "Black Swan"

Actually, there is more than enough time. There's plenty of time. We just waste it on a fascinating fight against "problems" and meaningless meetings.

Richard Koch.

In the first rule, we talked about the fact that more and more companies choose the policy of continuous improvement. These improvements concern business processes, technologies, approaches... But why not add another important aspect to it - the improvement of themselves...

yourself?

In my companies, it is a good tradition to write daily reports. Previously, this rule applied to all employees without exception. Now it has changed a bit: three categories of people write daily reports:

◆ employees on probation;

◆ remote employees;

◆ employees who have changed positions within the company and acquired new functions.

The algorithm is simple: finish work - write a report and then close the laptop lid.

Why do I and other managers need this? Does this smell like bureaucracy and unnecessary formalities? Not at all. A daily report is the best way to quickly and timely assess your own efficiency and productivity during the day.

What does it look like? Every ward in a tsk manager has his or her own task called "Daily reports (first name and last name)". In addition to the employee himself, there is a manager of that person. When an employee sits down at 9 a.m., he immediately opens this task and holds it in a separate tab in his browser. There, he writes down each new task he is working on. Going on to the next one, he writes down how long the previous one took.

In front of each task, the employee inserts a link to it. So, the manager can see exactly what the ward did. We have written communication, so that all steps of the executors are recorded in the tasks.

By six pm we have a list of tasks and the time that the employee has invested in them. After the list, each report has mandatory lines to update day by day:

◆ start of the working day;

◆ end of the business day;

◆ working hours;

◆ hours of processing.

Every evening the top manager receives reports from his immediate wards. He looks at what they have been doing all day and how much time they have invested in it.

Why is this necessary? A clear value for the employee himself. During the day, while he jumps from task to task, he cannot evaluate his performance. But at the end of the day, he says: "Yeah, today, I spent a whole hour helping a colleague prepare a report, although it is not my task. And here I spent a whole three hours stretching what I could do in two".

The manager also draws conclusions by studying the employee's report. He sees what his client is doing. He sees how quickly a person copes with the same task in a certain period - month, for example. This works well with newcomers. From their daily reports, one can judge their progress. Also, from the employee's report, the manager judges his or her workload and understands that he or she can be delegated in the near future and with what he or she should wait.

My daily reports are strict. I myself am in the tasks of some employees who are in direct contact with me. If for some reason I do not receive a report by the end of the day, I will be penalized. If I don't send the report on time, you might as well buy the whole office some fruit in the morning, publicly declare that you have broken the rule and undertake not to do so again. This is an example of a "fine" for violating the general rule, which we agreed on in advance.

Just once is enough for an employee to learn a lesson. It is inconvenient to admit your mistake in front of your colleagues. And after such public demotivation, he would rather stick a reminder sticker on his monitor than forget it again and fall under the penalty.

Punishment for failure to comply with the rules is a separate topic in the HR sphere. If you are interested in this rule, you can choose your reception. One of the popular is Bart Simpson's method. When an employee breaks the rule, he should write the phrase "I broke the rule, but I will not do it again" three hundred times on paper during his non-working hours. And in some offices, for misconduct, the employee must wear a funny hat and sit in it until the end of the day. This is called a "hat of delinquency". In general, as long as the owner maintains discipline in the company, he has a great platform for self-expression.

How else do you track efficiency? One of my companies has a rule to "turn off noise". Each employee turns off notifications to all social networks in his or her smartphone and then shows his or her colleague the settings. Of course, an employee can leave notifications for the resource he or she is connected to. When I ask my team to disable notifications, I don't mean a total ban on smartphones.

The essence of this rule is not to be distracted by the constant flashing of the display. These innocent seconds rip the wards out of the process, and then they need a few minutes to concentrate again. The main thing to understand about messages is that they must not dictate conditions. Employees check social networks when they have time, not every two seconds as soon as the screen lights up.

With regard to "noise", there is another way to check your effectiveness. To do this, an employee must write down each of his actions within three working days. Not only the working one, but any action at all. How many times I checked the social networks, brewed coffee, talked to a colleague, how long I talked on the phone. In the end, he will see his bad habits and understand what he should work on.

185

Without the daily reports of certain employees, I do not represent work in our companies. It is so convenient and demonstrative, that I recommend you to introduce this rule too! Run it in test mode for a month. I wonder if your idea of employees' work will match reality. Even if not, your team will have the opportunity to get even better. It's in your hands!

What gives the rule

"Keep statistics of tasks completed and evaluate personal effectiveness!"

◆ Helps an employee evaluate their performance and understand what they really invest time in.

◆ Allows managers to assess the load of their sub-stations and see their progress.

◆ Disciplines employees, encourages them to be more responsible for working time and less distracted.

Twenty-sixth rule

People come to the company and leave the manager!

Become the kind of manager you'd like to be.

Does your office policy meet the needs of your employees and their wishes? Knowing what makes your employees happy will not only increase productivity and motivation, but also reduce the number of layoffs.

Neil Lebowitz.

Every night, ninety-five percent of my company's total assets are driven home by car. My task is to create such working conditions that the next morning all these people have a desire to go back. The creativity they bring to the company creates a competitive advantage.

James Goodnight.

Have you noticed that I've never used the words in this book for "subordinate" and "boss"? It's not that I have a limited supply of synonyms. I just threw these words out of my vocabulary long ago and use them only in a negative context. Why is that? Because the "boss - subordinate" model is a relationship that I do not want to see in my companies.

This applies directly to rule number twenty-six. When a company's CEO appoints a new person to a management position, he or she focuses on his or her work capabilities. What do I mean? A manager is appointed someone who will be able to achieve the department's goals, optimize the work of his team, bring results to the company. Pragmatic, isn't it?

But many owners and managers forget that the emotional comfort of employees is a significant part of their efficiency. People will do more in less time if they work in a friendly atmosphere. But who provides this comfort? The company, the HR department, colleagues? In many ways, yes, but still the manager plays a crucial role.

Have you ever read the feedback of former employees of any company? One of the most common reasons for leaving is...

"didn't get along with the manager." Behind this correct formulation hides a whole range of negative emotions that employees experience day after day if they are "lucky" to work with a bad manager.

When an applicant comes to a company, he knows only what he saw in the text of the vacancy and what he noticed on the way to the recruiter's office. The vacancy is a kind of commercial offer, which indicates the main benefits of possible cooperation with the company. Salary, insurance, vacation, free swimming pool, HR chips - it's great. But that's not all.

When an employee accepts a "commercial offer" and comes to the company, he is immersed in the work. And here, the immediate supervisor comes to the fore in interaction. If he is not inclined to develop his employees, to listen to them, the efforts of the company and HR-department are leveled off.

Now the list of requirements to potential managers of my companies has grown considerably. In addition to professional qualities, no less important features have been added: emotional intelligence, the ability to listen, loyalty to colleagues. It is important that the manager listens to his employees and gives them what motivates them in time.

Of course, there are companies that think differently:

- We "squeeze out" the employees. We do not have a goal to leave them for a long time. The main thing is that during their work with us they give their best to realize our goals.

This position has a right to exist, but there are some nuances. It is usually found in large corporations in highly competitive positions. Employees are aware of these conditions because they want to gain experience in this particular company and write an impressive line on their resume. Yet, for the average small and medium-sized business, this model of team relations is not the most successful. A company is effective when the management and the team are in mutually beneficial conditions. The company achieves its goals with the help of its employees. And employees achieve their goals with the help of the company. What goals can the employee have? Professional development, new responsibility, promotion. If the manager ignores these goals, the employee will leave.

When I realized this, I became more selective in the selection of managers. I also began to pay more attention to their development. A manager must be mature enough to become a mentor for his employees. So, I ask a question to all my tops:

- If you were an employee, would you like to work with yourself?

Pay attention to the situation in your company. Analyze which department your employees leave most often. Conduct individual interviews or anonymous questionnaires with them. There are many ways to find out what kind of people are running your team. The main thing is to do it.

The efficiency of an employee depends on his emotional state. The emotional state is strongly influenced by the manager. If he behaves authoritatively, suppresses initiative, does not enter the employee's position, does not give him time and is not interested in his goals, it will be difficult for the employee to work. He will not be able to give a good result. And you know what else? His attitude towards his manager will spread all over the company. Because of a bad relationship with one management representative, he will automatically dislike all other colleagues in high positions. This means that he will sabotage the rules, not accept innovations. And he can also infect his colleagues with these sentiments.

Of course, you have to ask yourself a question about working with yourself, not only the tops, but also yourself. From time to time, and I do it. And it motivates me to develop: to study people, learn to understand them and interact with them. This is an ongoing process that should accompany the activities of any manager who is interested in a long-term and effective relationship with his team.

Above, I wrote that most often employees quit because of their managers. But there is another law: the employees often stay in the company because of their managers. I know many examples when the management could not create super comfortable conditions for their team. They had not the best office, not the highest salaries, but the employees were still interested in this job. That's because they believed in their leaders.

And it's true: people feel when they get into an environment where they are appreciated. Especially people who have already had a negative experience with an overly authoritarian boss. Therefore, every owner and manager have a choice. He may not bother selecting top managers, and then his company will become that "negative experience" for many employees. Or he can take up this issue and then his company will be an ideal place to work.

You also have this choice. And if you are interested in the second option, I recommend you to implement this rule and study your tops more closely. Be an example for them!

What gives the rule

"People come into the company and leave. from the manager! Be the kind of manager you'd like to be."

◆ Supports the emotional comfort of employees.

◆ Improves their effectiveness.

◆ In the future forms employee's loyalty to the whole company, which starts with the loyalty to the immediate superior.

◆ Reduces staff turnover.

Twenty-seventh rule

Always be a "company lawyer": protect the interests of your manager and your colleagues!

If you care about your own reputation, deal only with people who have decent qualities,

for it's better to be alone than in a bad company.

George Washington.

A few rules ago we partially addressed the issue of the company's reputation. Let us dwell on it in more detail. As an owner I understand very well what it is like to build a company and invest part of myself in it. It sounds pathetic, but isn't it? An owner builds a company on the foundation of his values. And recruits' people on the same principle: do they meet these values, are they ready to divide them in order to fulfill the mission of the company? By investing so much energy in his brainchild, the Owner of the business, of course, wants to... the people around him perceived his company accordingly.

It's not just the way other people will see the brand. It's important what kind of people the businessman surrounds himself with. Take me, for example. When I hire an employee and he undergoes a probationary period, I confirm that we will now spend some period of our lives in close cooperation. He will achieve his goals within the company and the company will achieve its goals with his help.

To do this, the company invests resources in people. It allocates money for his training, takes care of his emotional comfort, etc. This is because the new employee and the company have chosen each other. It goes without saying that the management does not allow even the thought that in this respect the ward will allow himself to be gossiped and criticized by the company outside.

But what if everything is not perfect in the organization? How can the employees maintain a friendly attitude and a good mood if they are not allowed to speak out? The answer is one: we need to create an environment within the company where any question can be discussed.

Who is a lawyer? This is the person who is always on the client's side. When we ask employees to be lawyers for the company, we expect their full support. But shouldn't a lawyer discuss his client's issues? Yes, he can. But only with the client himself.

It's exactly the same idea. An employee may disagree with the management's decision or with an individual colleague. He has a legal right to do so. And he can express his disagreement to a colleague or manager with whom he does not agree.

But in no case should the employee express his disagreement with the manager in public: in front of his colleagues, team, at general meetings. It would seem that they are all their own. In reality, however, this action reduces the credibility of the manager and shows everyone the disloyalty of the employee.

I think you share the view that employees should not carry dirt from the hut and criticize the manager and the company in front of other colleagues and outsiders. Of course, this has a negative impact on reputation. But there is another consequence of such actions, which affects the company's performance badly.

What am I talking about? An employee may disagree with management and its decisions. In order to resolve a problem that concerns him/her, he/she can come to his/her manager and talk to him/her personally, in a respectful manner. In this case, he will deal with what is bothering him.

But if the best thing this man can come up with is to go and complain, what conclusion can be drawn about him? That he belongs to the category of people I call the complainants. They are happy to criticize and spread the problem, but do not want to solve it. The conclusion is that they like the very position of disagreement. In this case, the manager must answer the question of whether he or she needs such people on the team.

You have put so much effort into your work that your business develops. Yes, the people in the team are not robots, so the human factor cannot be excluded. Be cautious: create in advance in the company such conditions, when the human factor will manifest itself without negative consequences. Then your like-minded people will not mind the title of "company lawyers". Good luck with implementation!

What gives the rule

"Always be a "company lawyer": protect the interests of your manager and your colleagues!"

◆ The owner is confident that his nesting.

the company's forces will not be devalued by the gossip of his own employees.

◆ Employees solve their problems through dialogue with the person who can solve them.

◆ At external events, employees will try to talk about the company and their supervisor well.

Twenty-eighth rule

Plan your day from tonight.

Release your Inbox and Today folder at the end of the day in your management system.

My first boat, as the reader already knows, I made such a huge size, not having calculated in advance whether I would be able to launch it, that I was forced to leave it at the site of the construction as a monument to my stupidity, which should constantly remind me that you should be smarter from now on.

Danielle Defeau "Robinson Crusoe."

I once asked all the employees in the company's general chat room to drop off screenshots of empty "Inbox" and "Today" folders in their manager before they went home. Why did I do that? Was it my whim or was it me by someone with a sophisticated method of control?

Actually, it's just a way to control written communication. As you may recall, the rule without discipline does not work. My method above is discipline. This is how I and other managers can be sure that the rule of written communication and good planning is maintained.

Each management system has its own blocks and sections. Nevertheless, they have the same logic. There are incoming tasks and there are several folders where they can be moved depending on priority and time.

We work in one of these task management systems. Our HR specialists have created a whole document with rules of using this task force. But the point is that each employee distributes all incoming tasks at once, as they come in. Those that he has to perform on the same day, he must first move to the folder "Today". The rest should be packed in other folders. The main thing is that they do not accumulate in the Inbox.

I don't insist on order because I'm a pedant and I don't tolerate messing with other people's computers. I insist on it because this approach teaches employees to perform their tasks and responsibility for them in a timely manner. If a task is expected today, it must be completed on the same day. If the task is in the Inbox, you must move it to the right folder.

At the end of the day, the Inboxes should be empty, let alone empty. Otherwise they lose their meaning. An employee cannot stretch tasks that are designed for a couple of hours by several days.

It's easy to make a heap in your task book. If you don't clear up new tasks at the same time, you may accumulate hundreds of them. But a hundred tasks in "Incoming" is not a reason to be proud of what kind of employee is in demand. It's a reason to review his time management skills.

I will tell you right away: I have two-digit numbers in my Inbox folder. But I'm not a direct performer. As an owner in most of them, I am added only to the approval. My role in such cases is to approve or not approve the decisions of employees. In doing so, I still maintain order and use the system as required by the rules. I expect the same from the team.

Along with the ritual of releasing two employee folders, another evening procedure awaits - planning the next day. Why exactly in the evening? Of course, there will be no less time for this process in the evening than in the morning. That's not the point here. It is easier to plan tomorrow night from the evening, because the employee immediately understands his load and can distribute the forces in advance.

In addition, morning time is considered more productive for most people. In the evening it is better to do mechanical work that does not require much energy.

Surely you think: why take such a trifle into a separate corporate rule? Isn't it enough to have instructions for using a task-management system or an online calendar? It's not enough. The aim is not to teach employees how to push buttons. Through this rule, I want to convey the message to the team: it's easy to beat yourself up with tasks. One hundred, two hundred tasks - in a couple of weeks the Inbox will accumulate any number. But there is nothing of value or illustrative in it.

The real indicator of an employee's usefulness to the company is his productivity. If he is able to do what is required of him and does not allow chaos, he is a valuable employee.

If you agree with me, help your employees with time management and planning. Sometimes "Be organized" requests are not enough. Sometimes you have to show the team exactly how to achieve this. These specific rules and instructions will help your colleagues to discipline all systems and calendars. Be specific and then your team will progress faster!

What gives the rule

"Plan your day from tonight. Release your Inbox and Today folder at the end of the day. in the management system."

◆ Does not allow rubble in employee work plans.

◆ Maintains written communication discipline.

◆ Teaches competent planning.

◆ Shows colleagues what the company expects from them and what they really appreciate. Helps to navigate in a new tradition of written negotiations and online planning.

Twenty-ninth rule

The Company does not evaluate and reward an employee for the processes, but for the results he or she achieves.

The productivity of a working group seems to depend on how its members see their goals in relation to the organization's goals.

Ken Blanchard.

No, it's not deja vu. You've already seen the rule about DDS - the result of an employee's activity - but now we're not going to talk about much else. We will continue to develop the theme of results and so on, what the company expects from its team.

I agree: this rule really echoes the one you read before. It says that every employee must have the main result of all his activities, on which he can concentrate his attention. What is this rule about? About the fact that any DDS is achieved through dozens of tasks, and in these tasks, you should just as well focus on the result.

Every employee should understand that the management does not take into account his or her sacrifices. We had an employee who spent the night in the office. Literally. Worked until the night and then fell asleep in a pillow chair. Seems so zealous... Must have been some kind of natural "employee of the month." But in fact, it was the other way around.

This man did much less than his colleagues with an eight-hour day's work. And if we were to present the team's success in the form of a progress table, his name would be at the bottom.

What do we have? A man spends his time destroying his health for the company. But in the end, his performance is lower than that of everyone else, and he is dragging his debts a month ago, when everyone is already planning goals for six months ahead. This story teaches us two things:

1. It is necessary to constantly focus on the result and not to do unnecessary things.

2. A heap at work and forced overnights in the office are not an indicator of efficiency and value for the company. Rather, it is the opposite.

In your company, people do not have to go to extremes to make you feel the need to introduce this rule. But I am sure that you still know what it's like to work with "processors". These people work harder than others and there is no result. The management doesn't accept this approach to work - it's been dealt with. What to do then? Based on the fact that managers should be mentors for their mentees, they should offer the team help. If the solution is shown, the goal can be reached much faster. The goal is to make employees were focusing on the result.

I can offer a solution that we periodically use in my companies. It is a tool called "Monthly targets". Yes, everything is brilliant (or effective) easy! How does it work? On the first day of the month, each employee creates a mental map of their main objectives for the next month. There, he adds seven to ten tasks, which in terms of time and priority are included in the next thirty days.

Next to each task, he draws a scale with a graduation from zero to ten. You need it to paint over the task as it progresses. When the mental map sketch is ready, the employee shows it to his manager. He checks it and, if necessary, corrects it. Taking into account the remarks, the ward corrects the document and prints out the ready version.

What's next? Next, he goes to a special booth hanging in the office and attaches his printed map with targets there. By hand, he writes on his leaflet that he undertakes to fulfill all the planned goals within this month. And so, every evening, all employees go to the stand and mark the progress on the maps - paint bars next to the tasks.

What do we have? Month after month, the whole team is focused on its results. We ask them to do it, and they do it. They don't need to make an effort to find the ultimate goal of the task. They see a leaf with goals, and they achieve them.

The element of publicity is very important here. Employees do not mark progress in their task, where no one else sees it. They do this on a common stand, on the office wall. It involves not just responsibility for the result, but a competition with colleagues: "How is this? It has already had so many tasks painted over! How am I worse?"

Publicity + healthy competition = guarantee that the rule will be followed. I recommend that you use this formula if you decide to implement this rule. And in relation to other innovations, it works no worse.

You can use the personal goals of the department for a month to shift employees' focus to results. You can complement and refine this method or take some other. That's not the point. If you understand the importance of effective thinking among employees, tell them what you expect. Not the process, but the result. Not the victims, but the result. Not the rework, the result. I am sure that when you explain it in simple words, employees will listen to you. That's what I want you to do!

What gives the rule

"The Company does not evaluate and reward an employee for the processes, but for the results he achieves."

◆ Brings to the team what management expects of it. Brings clarity to the approach to work: not sacrifice, but result.

◆ Helps employees see results in their daily routine.

◆ Shows how to achieve your EPR, for which the company pays its salary, through small tasks.

Thirtieth rule

Work efficiently and effectively. Offer simple solutions for complex tasks.

The problem is that we try to solve the simplest questions in a cunning way, and therefore make them unusually difficult.

We need to find a simple solution.

Let's see the situation. You had your assistant drink you a train ticket. At the end of the day he sent a report on his tasks, where there are not many points. One of them: "Buying a train ticket is four hours." When you asked why an employee spent half a day doing this simple task, he answered:

- Well, what about it? I packed up, went to the train station, stood in line and went back to the office.

That's an honest answer. What would seem to resent? Do you have a result? Yes, there is. Did the employee complete the task on time? On time. Then what's wrong? The fact is that the assistant focused only on the result, but did not think about efficiency. In four hours, he could have done much more.

What does it mean to work efficiently? It means to achieve the result with the least amount of resources: time, financial, human. The goal is not only to achieve the result. The goal is also to achieve as many results as possible in one unit of time. To achieve more, but not at the expense of quality.

How could the issue of a wait-and-see ticket be dealt with more effectively? Elementary - to buy it online. Perhaps the employee had such an idea. But he was stopped by the fact that you gave him cash, and there was no money for it. But he could have gone to the nearest terminal and transferred the money to his account to solve the problem online. He could also have booked a ticket or even sent a courier to pick him up. There are many options to solve the problem more efficiently.

Buying a ticket is a simple example. Every day much more complex processes take place in the company. But I am sure that many of them can be made more effective. Every day the company buys equipment, negotiates with partners, serves customers, orders services from contractors.

I urge my employees to ask themselves a question before taking up the task:

- How to solve this task in such a way as to save your resources and those of the company, but not to reduce the quality of the result?

The most common solutions are. People suddenly find discounts, defend their interests in negotiations, learn about new technologies and use them. Thus, employees do not waste energy on unnecessary actions and thus have time to do everything planned.

This rule may not be useful for a company which does not care what it invests in. If management is willing to allocate unlimited amounts of money for salaries and expenses and does not require compliance with a certain norm, then it is quite possible to do without it. However, most business owners and executives have a reasonable approach to their budget, time and effort. This means that they will definitely think about efficiency.

On the example of buying a train ticket, we have figured out how to save time and effort of employees. An equally important topic is the preservation of the company's financial resources. I teach my team how to save, if possible. Being part of a company, people are also interested in investing it rationally.

Yes, you can take the allocated budget and chic - buy with all the money equipment in the most popular store with a markup. Or you can search a little and save money on training. In general, a purely family approach that cultivates in the team an understanding of its role in the company and responsibility for its finances.

It's just not enough to appeal to the conscience of employees. It's better to motivate it. For me, the best option for motivation is a competent combination of financial incentives, an element of competition and public praise. How do we motivate employees whose job is to buy something for the company? We offer them to work in a regime of constant price reductions.

What does this mean? If the IT department constantly buys the same laptops, each time you need to look for them at a lower price. The lower price is fixed, and the next purchase should be even cheaper. Needless to say, this should not affect the quality of the product.

The same is done by other departments that regularly buy something with company money. The main motivation to constantly look for cheaper options is the bonus for saving money. On some positions, the price will sooner or later stop dropping - a fact. But the company is constantly updated and added products, equipment. New opportunities to find an effective solution appear.

In the previous chapter, I called on you to shift the focus of your employees to the result. This is a major step for the company and its team. For many, it is a fundamentally different approach to work. It is a great merit of the management - when it seeks from the team effective thinking.

But that's not all. It is necessary to work not only effectively, but also efficiently - with the least amount of resources spent. Let your employees know that you don't have to go out of your way to solve the problem. Give them some sympathy for simple and effective solutions. The results of their work will then be even more valuable.

What gives the rule

"Work efficiently and effectively. Offer simple solutions for complex tasks."

◆ Saves the company time, effort and money.

◆ Allows businesses to achieve more in one time.

◆ Develops team awareness in the use of its resources and those of the company.

Thirty-first rule

Do not allow inaccurate or unverified information relating to employees and company activities to be disseminated.

- I think about who you're talking about.

- Does anybody else have any idea besides you?

- The whole team.

- The information is in good order!

Dialogue from the "Official Affair".

In the XIX century, Belgian journalist Robert Cornelissen decided to check how easy it is to fool readers. He came up with a small story about the greediness of ducks and printed it in a newspaper. It was about a duck that ate nineteen of its "relatives". As a journalist and expected, readers took the news for a clean coin and then discussed it for a long time. Later, Cornelissen confessed that he was joking. So, according to one of the versions the expression "newspaper duck."

The history of journalism knows hundreds of examples when newspaper ducks and unverified information were distributed so widely that they became indisputable facts for people. If deception was exposed, journalists would ask their readers for forgiveness. But the irony is that apologies have far less coverage than pseudo-donors.

Rumors always diverge at an astonishing rate. Even if they do not sound in TV news, but in the smoke of a small company. And the more scandalous and madder these rumors are, the more active people are in spreading them.

Imagine a situation: an employee of yours notices a colleague after work walks up to an unfamiliar car and gives the driver a product that your company sells.

"Wow, it seems that my colleague is selling something behind the back of the management," thinks the employee.

The next morning, he tells this story to a friend. At the end of the day, the whole office jokes about "it turns out there's a leftist among us". Later, the rumor reaches the employee and his manager, and it turns out that he has not engaged in any fraudulent activities. He simply handed over the goods personally to the client, because he was asked to do so by his manager.

The conflict seemed to have been resolved. But it's not that simple. Like the public apology for misinformation, this new information does not reach everyone. Part of the staff continues to think badly of a colleague and, even if there are revealing false rumors, already treats him differently.

Rumors and gossip have a devastating effect. What do they threaten the company with?

Tainted reputation.

An employee who is the victim of speculation looks differently in the eyes of colleagues.

Decrease in efficiency.

As long as the employees discuss the news, they don't work. Time goes nowhere, the company loses money.

Lack of corporate culture.

If employees discuss their colleague behind his back and think it is normal, then the company has a weak corporate culture.

This last point is very important. In a company with a healthy microclimate and well-established corporate culture, employees do not spread rumors. And if they do, they know they are breaking the rule. When they gossip, they make a conscious choice: go against company values and management.

But what should employees do if they have seen what they think is obviously unfair? What to do if they want to know the truth? Let them get it from your leadership. It is necessary to create in a company such conditions so that the team knows who to go to first, before sharing speculations with others. The management has to say it openly:

- If you have doubts about something and want to find out the truth, talk to any top manager or HR specialist. In our company everything is honest, we do not hide anything from you.

It is important for our company to ensure transparency in this matter. Many employees are not by nature gossip. They are even guided by good intentions: "I will share my guess with a comrade to be more careful with this suspicious guy".

Well, it is better to create such a culture of relationships, when the team itself will reject such statements. If the corporate culture is strong, the employees themselves push out the numbers that are trying to get them into their own affairs.

Perhaps some workers will continue to gossip. These are the "employee viruses" that I have already told you about. It is only by giving the corporate rule that you can stop such behavior and explain that it is unacceptable.

In the eighteen years of Mir Weights' history, the HR department did not appear right away. That means it is never too late to start creating a corporate culture and new rules. This is their peculiarity - something can always be improved and supplemented. That is why I recommend you to implement this rule. Take care of the reputation and efficiency of your colleagues!

What gives the rule

"Do not allow inaccurate or unverified information relating to employees and company activities to be disseminated".

◆ Maintains a good reputation for its employees within and outside the company.

◆ Allows employees to invest energy in their work rather than in gossip and discussion.

◆ Provides transparency in the company and develops trust in management.

◆ Maintains a healthy corporate culture, which over time is less and less in need of specialists' reaction as it rejects "employees-viruses".

Thirty-second rule

The efficiency of the department is assessed by the weakest employee, and the development of the company depends on the quality of work of the weakest top manager.

I love the job: it captures me completely.

I can sit for hours and watch others work.

Jerome Flap Jerome.

Eliyahu Goldratt has a good book, "The Target." It's a business novel about how to solve problems in a company. The part of the company that prevents the whole business from developing is called the "narrow neck". Any company can potentially have its own "narrow neck" - such a pre-flooding machine in modern production, which reduces overall efficiency.

In the role of such a "machine tool" specific departments or staff members speak.

There are companies where everything seems to be good: production makes an excellent product, marketing leads many customers. But the company still does not sell the product, because the sales department does not do its job. For all the merits of most departments, a business does not get enough profit just because of one department.

The same thing happens within departments. Their "narrow necks" are weak employees, who are slow to level the work of other colleagues. And the department develops with the speed of such weak employees.

What should business owners and managers do? To constantly monitor the situation. The best indicators here are the numbers. For this purpose, it is necessary to set a specific measurable goal for each department on a monthly basis - the number of listed customers, profit, issued details, agreements with partners, etc. Those departments that do not systematically close their goals are the first in the list of suspected braking of the whole company.

It is just as easy to track weak employees. When all wards have KPIs, the results can be used to identify who is clearly lagging behind and pulling the whole department behind.

Remember, I have already cited this wording several times, which I have now put in a separate rule? This is because it is worth implementing it in conjunction with other rules and traditions. The main one is self-development and continuous learning. Yes, we tell employees that we will not tolerate their systematic bad results. But at the same time, we help them to constantly pump up their skills and gain knowledge.

Any "narrow neck" in a company is a potential for development. Look at the phenomenon from a different perspective. If even with braking departments or employees you somehow move, what happens if you remove these brakes? The main thing is not to be afraid of changes, not to be afraid to improve the usual course of things.

Previously, my companies had employees who did not want to work and hid behind the backs of more responsible colleagues. When I slowly started to implement the new rules, these employees immediately found themselves. I think there are people like that wherever there is no proper discipline. But any manager is capable of making a difference. It's an axiom rule - one of the right tools. Bring it to the team, and see how it reacts!

What gives the rule

"The efficiency of the department is evaluated by the weakest employee, and the development of the company depends on the quality of work of the weakest top manager".

◆ The team understands that imitation activity no longer works. Therefore, employees either improve and develop, or make room for new specialists.

◆ Management is aware that it is first necessary to improve the performance of the weakest department and then to work on improvements in others.

Thirty-third rule

There's nothing impossible. All you have to do is define the necessary resources - human, temporary, material.

Rule six "P": correct preliminary preparation prevents bad performance.

Brian Tracy.

"Luck" comes after careful preparation; "bad luck" is the result of negligence.

Robert Heinline.

Most of my managers I know agree that they are madly demotivated by employees' fear of new and complex tasks. For some reason, this is quite common behavior. Some good specialists are afraid to go beyond their business schemes and job descriptions. Need to send a letter to another city in one day? But usually, we send it in two days, it is impossible! Do you need to bring ten customers instead of five? But five is our ceiling, no more. That's clearly not what the manager wants to hear, is it?

At first glance, it might seem like the downside of the system business. When employees have clear business processes and instructions, their ability to look for nontrivial solutions is lost. But I think this is not a reason to become an opponent of systematization, but an incentive to improve the existing situation.

I suggest using this rule. What is it doing? It gradually changes the paradigm of thinking of employees. They do not say: "It is impossible". They answer the question: what can be done to solve the problem? What resources do we need to attract?

The catch is precisely that some employees do not allow themselves to think outside the box. For them, there is only such a norm and it must be followed. In fact, any task can be solved by simply reviewing the resources. Yes, it is not possible to deliver the letter in one day by standard mail. But it is possible to ask a private courier to do it. It is almost impossible to take five new specialists in a team without a staff recruiter, but it is quite real to transfer this order to a recruiting agency and close vacancies.

The longer I observe the market, the clearer I see an obvious trend: there is a growing demand for people with flexible thinking. A computer may not go beyond the instructions. But to orientate in an urgent and difficult situation under the power of a specialist with appropriate thinking.

Of course, if you immediately demand extraordinary solutions from your employees, they will get confused. Therefore, it is necessary to convey the following conviction to the team:

- Anything is possible. Any problem can be solved. No matter how real a task may seem at first sight, accept the idea that it is possible to accomplish it. It is only a question of the necessary resources. Ask yourself the question: "How many resources do I need? In this way, you will analyze the task, disassemble it into components. And already with a specific list of requirements, you will come to the manager. Make your request sound clear: "To complete the task, I need a, b, c, d". Be real experts. Look for ways to do it, not for reasons why it is impossible to do it.

Each employee must be sure that he or she is capable of accomplishing a complex task - it is enough to understand it. Toggle and feedback from him will sound many times more convincing:

- I have understood your catalog development task. I can create the layout and edit the description myself, but I need the designer's power to design it.

There is nothing fancy about this rule. I am not trying to convince my team members that they can break bricks with their heads and move trucks. I'm teaching them to think pragmatically. They have to take complex tasks and solve them in unpopular ways if the popular ones don't work. Within reason, of course. So, you can attract additional resources - human, material or temporary.

I advise you to implement this rule as well. But for your employees to believe that nothing is impossible, you must believe in it yourself.

What gives the rule

"There's nothing impossible. All we have to do is identify the necessary resources - human, temporal, material."

◆ Changes the paradigm of employee thinking from pessimistic to optimistic.

◆ Allows the company to become more efficient and in demand in the market through unconventional solutions.

Thirty-fourth rule

Notify your colleague that the information is accepted and received by any affirmative action or phrase.

A question that is not answered immediately is multiplied at an alarming rate.

Robert Rollins

Attentive readers have noticed: something similar they have already seen somewhere. Let me remind you where in rule number twelve.

It sounds like this: "Did you complete the task? Make sure the leader is familiar with the result."

As you remember, it said that the task is the responsibility of the performer. And he may think he completed the task to the end when he is satisfied that the leader has received the result. The performer is not just required to put tea on the table of the manager, but to put it with words:

- Here is your tea.

I agree, the rules are similar, but the thirty-fourth is different. It is no longer addressed to the performers of the task, and to the delegators. Imagine the situation: you wrote a message to an employee in the messenger asking him to reset the report to you at a specific time. At the appointed time, you sit and wait, but nothing comes. Then you go into the correspondence and see that the employee has not read your message and has not even appeared online.

A strange and unpleasant situation, you agree. The same can happen in an office where live communication and the joys of oral communication prevail. You can set a task for the employee, and he will safely miss your words.

Not on purpose, but simply because I didn't hear you talking to him.

To avoid such ridiculous misunderstandings, I have introduced a mandatory rule: the employee must always let the delegate know that he accepted the task. It doesn't matter what the confirmation is:

◆ nodded;

◆ said "Yeah"

- showed his thumb;

- said "okay."

- signed off for a messenger or a management system.

Any sign of involvement in the process will do. The main thing that the delegate understands is that the employee has accepted and understood the incoming information.

The rule is the simplest, and even ridiculous to implement it at the corporate level. It was funny to me too, until I saw a workflow being disrupted by such nonsense. Discussing the twelfth rule, we said that the performer could not consider the task completed until he reported it to the manager. In the thirty-fourth rule, we say that the delegator cannot consider the task completed unless he has received confirmation of its acceptance from the performer.

This rule is particularly relevant when you set many different tasks in the messenger to one employee within a short period of time.

It would be good to implement both of these rules. In this way, the parties insure each other, and the management calmly for the work process. If you are familiar with cases when an employee did not know that the task is already on him, implement this rule.

This way you will have more confidence that the employees will provide the result.

What gives the rule

"Notify your colleague that the information has been accepted and received by any affirmative action or phrase."

◆ Reduces the risk that the workflow will be disrupted by some ridiculous thing.

◆ Divides responsibility between the two sides of the task: shows what the delegate should do and what the responsible party should do.

◆ Adds clarity and literacy to the culture of interaction between employees.

Thirty-fifth rule

Give me quality feedback. We get what we focus our attention on.

It's often said that the motivation isn't long enough.

But the same thing happens with a refreshing shower, so it's recommended daily.

Zig Ziglar.

Look at what happens when we're concerned about a topic. If we want to buy a car and look at a certain model, we suddenly begin to notice it everywhere - on the roads, in advertising. No, no one has brought a dozen or two extra cars into town. It's just that we've focused on them.

It's the same with employees. When we scold and criticize them all the time, their subconscious takes out this algorithm: "Yeah, the manager pays attention to my work when I do it badly. So, to get his attention, I have to continue to attract him with a bad result".

Unfortunately, this is how it works. When I realized this, I started to praise my employees more often. I've been looking for actions that really make a person stand out.

But look at this thing. You probably know that constant praise, especially for simple actions, reduces a person's ability to solve serious tasks. Child psychologists do not recommend abusing the phrase "My little genius" if a child just counts to five.

No, I do not give up the idea that employees should be praised. However, I will make it clear that quality feedback must be given in a certain way. What am I talking about? It is easy to criticize an employee's work and stick his nose into mistakes. But will it have a positive effect on his self-esteem, efficiency and emotional state? Hardly.

I propose the following variant of qualitative feedback. You tell the employee that he has succeeded. Then you tell the employee that it can be improved. It's to improve, not to destroy it immediately and not to show it to anyone. Feedback in this format performs its main tasks:

◆ informs the employee of what he or she has done well and correctly so that he or she can repeat the correct action next time;

◆ explains what should be done differently next time, and how;

◆ maintains his working spirit and does not lower his self-esteem.

We take a big risk when we only tell an employee what he or she has done wrong. At the same time, it is very likely that the next time he or she will only focus on correcting mistakes, and that what has been done is correct. It is therefore important to give feedback on two things: what was good and what can be improved. In this way, the employee will remember his or her correct actions and repeat them next time, and replace the unsuccessful ones with improved ones.

No matter how badly an employee has done a task, there is always something to praise them for. Although I hope that you often get a generally good result, which simply requires some extra work. Still, here is an example of merit for which it is not a sin to give the employee credit:

◆ he does everything on time;

◆ he does the job quickly;

◆ he doesn't forget to unsubscribe from the management system;

◆ he's got an order on his desk;

◆ he gets the tasks right.

Always start giving qualitative feedback by saying what the employee did well.

What gives the rule

"Give quality feedback. We get what we focus on."

◆ Staff members achieve attention through praiseworthy actions and thus improve overall performance.

◆ The team is in a comfortable emotional state, which is why it works effectively.

◆ With quality feedback, employees are aware of their growth areas, but find the strength and spirit to correct mistakes and work on themselves.

◆ Employees understand what they are doing well and will try to repeat these actions in the future.

Thirty-sixth rule

If the main priority of the task is urgency, it is better to complete the task on time (even if not by one hundred and two percent) than to break the agreed deadlines and not to provide the result at all.

The rule is simple: do everything not at the last moment, but as soon as possible.

Michael Weller.

Remember the moment at the interview when the candidate answers a question about shortcomings: "You know, I'm a terrible perfectionist"?

Everyone understands that's a socially acceptable answer. The applicant speaks in such a way as to please the employer and not to reveal his secrets more easily.

Well, the thirty-sixth rule applies to cases where "creepy perfectionism" from the interview is true.

It is not for nothing that I have mentioned many times the importance of deadlines and objectives, as well as the importance of correct acceptance of the task. This is because it is the special conditions of the task that determine how the employee will perform it. And if the task is needed "yesterday", it is necessary to concentrate on speed.

Any result can be brought to perfection. If you want, you can perform a task other than a hundred and two - two hundred and two percent. But how does this desire relate to the real situation? If you have a meeting with partners tomorrow and you need a presentation the day after tomorrow, it will lose its meaning. You just won't need it.

I'm all for the extra result. And I'm still a hundred and two percent. I hope that in a company with good planning and well-established communication between employees, most tasks are designed to be able to refine and improve.

However, even the mother administrators have mega-tasks. And then those deadlines come to the fore, because the task is relevant to the deadline. The way is a spoon to lunch! Healthy perfectionism - good quality. The key word is "healthy." If a person has a nervous seizure due to the fact that he passes the presentation with extra space, it is not very good. Especially when the office is already sitting managers with partners and waiting for this very presentation.

If deadlines are really important, you should inform the performer immediately. Many management systems have special notes for these presentations. It is high time to use them.

Explain to your staff the elusive line between a task with a bright red deadline and a task that is two weeks away from the deadline. Any employee, including a perfectionist, will adapt to these circumstances. But the rule will help the team. Implement it, and be happy when your team copes with even "yesterday's" tasks. Remember: better on time than super quality.

What gives the rule

"If the main priority of the task is urgency, it is better to complete the task on time (even if not by one hundred and two percent) than to break the agreed deadlines and not to provide the result at all".

◆ Explains to employees the importance of correctly accepting the task and its details.

◆ Teaches how to prioritize between over-results and deadlines according to the task at hand.

Rule thirty-seven

Remember, understand and adhere to the company's temperature regime in the form of three "P's" - Principles, Rules and Paradigms of Work.

Observance of all rules is the basis for the effective functioning of the company.

The secret to moving forward steadily is to take the first step.

The secret of the first step is to break down complex, seemingly insurmountable tasks into simple and feasible ones, and start with the very first. The secret of success is the permanence of the goal.

Mark Twain.

Congratulations to you! You have learned all the rules, principles and paradigms that keep a healthy temperature inside my companies and the companies of my graduates who own my business. And now the most interesting thing: all the innovations will work with the right strength and efficiency, if you bring the case to life.

to the end and implement them in all the parameters.

What am I talking about? There are several criteria that guarantee that the rules will prove useful:

◆ Rules should be implemented from top to bottom: from owner to employee.

First of all, the rules must be accepted by top managers and all management. If these employees understand their usefulness, they will be able to convey the importance of the rules to their teams. If the top managers decide that the rules are an empty idea, the owner and the manager will get new problems within the team.

◆ There must be responsible people in the company who will monitor compliance with the rules.

It is not allowed to enter rules for the sake of a tick. If they are not followed in practice, people will lose confidence in the management and will take the rules seriously. We don't tell employees to come at 9 am to take this into account and do it their own way? We set clear conditions and check everyone through the pass system. So corporate rules need to be controlled too.

◆ The company must provide sanctions for violations of the rules.

These do not have to be fines. The main thing is for violators and their colleagues to be immediately informed that they have violated the rules. If they do not do so, discipline will suffer.

It is important to note that the application of sanctions should not be selective. People will be outraged: why do some people get away with it and not others? Therefore, make sure that you punish your wards in time and with your own methods for not following the rules.

◆ As a person in a leadership position, you must follow these rules and be an example.

You can make children read books as much as you want. But they will never do that if parents are in front of them with a tablet and a smartphone. The same principle works with corporate rules. They go from the top, and they should do it from the top. If you believe in the rules, start with yourself - and set an example!

That's it. Now all you have to do is print these rules as a poster and hang them on the walls of the office. Let your employees see them, study them, get used to them. You can also get these rules in video format to embed them in the adaptation system for new employees or to train the whole team. To do this, scan the QR code at the end of each chapter.

One day, these rules will be part of your strong corporate culture. One day, they will make you even more efficient and improve your performance. I only wish you that this "someday" will come as soon as possible!

P. S. So that we can continue to meet, here are my coordinates. With their help, you can receive updates, communicate with me and your like-minded people from the business world. Just point your camera at the QR code and open my social networking pages. Sign up, add to your friends.

See you later!

Peter Sinegub,

Manage teams through chaos, before chaos managed you.

37 rules of effective team.